Spirits of Palestine

D1613534

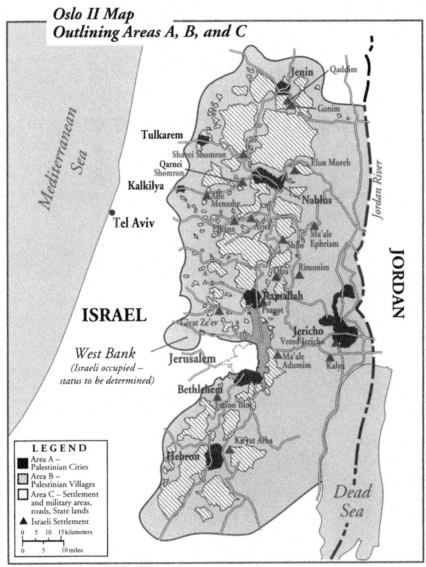

Oslo II Map
Outlining Areas A, B, and C

Jenin
Qadim
Ganim

Mediterranean Sea

Tulkarem
Sha'rei Shomron
Qarnei Shomron
Elon Moreh
Kalkilya
Alfe Menashe
Nablus

Tel Aviv
Elkana
Ariel
Ma'ale Ephriam
Shilo

Ofra
Rimonim

ISRAEL
Ramallah
Psagot

Givat Ze'ev
Jericho
Vered Jericho

West Bank
(Israeli occupied –
status to be determined)
Jerusalem
Ma'ale Adumim
Kalya

Bethlehem
Etzion Bloc

Kiryat Arba
Hebron

Jordan River

JORDAN

Dead Sea

LEGEND
■ Area A –
Palestinian Cities
▨ Area B –
Palestinian Villages
☐ Area C – Settlement
and military areas,
roads, State lands
▲ Israeli Settlement

0   5   10   15 kilometers
0   5   10 miles

Source: Yediot Aharonot, October 6, 1995

Spirits of Palestine

Gender, Society, and Stories of the Jinn

Celia E. Rothenberg

LEXINGTON BOOKS
Lanham • Boulder • New York • Toronto • Oxford

LEXINGTON BOOKS

Published in the United States of America
by Lexington Books
An imprint of The Rowman & Littlefield Publishing Group, Inc.
4501 Forbes Boulevard, Suite 200, Lanham, Maryland 20706

PO Box 317
Oxford
OX2 9RU, UK

British Library Cataloguing in Publication Information Available

Library of Congress Cataloging-in-Publication Data

Rothenberg, Celia, 1970–
    Spirits of Palestine : gender, society, and the stories of the jinn / Celia E. Rothenberg.
        p. cm.
    Includes bibliographical references and index.
    ISBN 0-7391-0642-2 (cloth : alk. paper) — ISBN 978-0-7391-0643-3
    1. Artas—Social life and customs. 2. Palestinian Arabs—Social life and customs.
3. Jinn. I. Title.
DS110.A74R68 2004
956.95'3—dc22   2004018661

Printed in the United States of America

For my mother
and for Rob

Contents

Figures

Acknowledgments

I must first acknowledge the debt and gratitude I owe to the villagers of Artas. Without their good humor and support this book would not have been possible. Special thanks must go to Musa Sanad, to my hosts, and to my research assistant. I must also thank Renée-Anne Gutter for the countless ways in which she has assisted me during my trips to Israel and the West Bank over the years.

The institutions that funded this research and the time to write about it include: The Research Institute for the Study of Man (Landes Award for Field Research), the University of Toronto (including support from the University of Toronto Open Fellowship, the Melissa J. Knauer Award, and the Lorna Marshall Doctoral Fellowship), and the Harry Frank Guggenheim Foundation (Guggenheim Dissertation Award). Massey College provided a warm and welcoming atmosphere upon my return to Toronto from the West Bank and assisted me in covering the costs of living and attending a number of conferences related to my work. A postdoctoral fellowship from the Rockefeller Foundation allowed me to explore avenues of research that served to deepen my discussion of the material discussed here. McMaster University's Department of Religious Studies and Health Studies Programme have been supportive as I worked to complete the project. The support of each of these institutions is gratefully acknowledged here.

I also thank Ellen Badone, Janice Boddy, Dianne Rothenberg, and the anonymous reviewers of the earlier versions of this manuscript for their critical comments and support. I feel fortunate to have Serena Leigh Krombach, Sheila-Katherine Zwiebel, and Jason Hallman of Lexington Books as my editors. Their careful attention to detail and pleasant natures made my publishing experience memorable.

Finally, I thank Rob, Joshua, and Adam Shenker for being exactly as they are.

McMaster University
Spring 2004

Chapter One

Introduction

Last night, the women and girls slept on the roof of the house to try to catch a cool summer evening breeze — some relief from the unbearable heat that seemed to have saturated even the walls and floors inside the house. The men had the roof the night before, so the women of my household and our female neighbors slept last night on our roof, the smoothest one for sleeping. As we tossed and turned, waiting to fall asleep in the heat, my neighbor turned to me and asked me in a whisper if I had heard what happened to another neighbor of ours. I hadn't, I told her. Well, my neighbor continued, it seemed that this young woman had been possessed [literally, "worn"] by a jinn [spirit] just the week before. The spirit had made her act crazy, scream, and hit those who came near her, and even spoke through the young woman in a language no one could understand but with a few words of Hebrew scattered in. (Field notes, September, 1995)

This book is an ethnography of the social lives of women and men and their stories of interaction with the jinn, or spirits, in the Muslim village of Artas, about two miles southwest of Bethlehem in the Palestinian West Bank. I lived in Artas with a family for fourteen months (July 1995 to September 1996) and was privileged to become intimately familiar with the lives of the women in the households in my neighborhood. After I had been in Artas for nearly three months, I recorded the exchange above. I soon decided to pursue these stories and to work to unravel their meanings. In the pages that follow, I examine stories of spirit possession, probing them for what they reveal about the nature of social relationships in village life and about villagers' experiences of power stemming from those relationships.

1

"TO WEAR" A JINN

The commonly used Arabic phrase "to wear a jinn" suggests an important indigenous framework for the interpretation of jinn stories, a framework that relies on the publicly recognized and symbolic significance of the jinn for its shades of meaning. When possessed, a person is said "to be worn by" or "to wear" (from the verb *labisa*,[1] meaning to wear or to dress) a jinn. Looking closely at this phrase and its referents is a good starting point for a discussion of the jinn and possession experiences. Most obviously, women "wear" their clothes; by saying, "I'm going to dress" one often means putting on nicer clothes than one is currently wearing. These actions are publicly oriented: One *dresses* (often nicely) for other people. A woman who is properly covered is respectable: Thus the Arabic phrase to a single woman of marriageable age, "May you be covered by a husband." The outward personal appearance of preferably new, stylish, clean, unwrinkled, and modest clothes signifies an honorable social self and successful family. Just as the area in front of a house is understood to be an externalization of the areas that are generally not seen by most villagers (discussed further in chapter 3), so a woman's appearance is an externalization of her social self, a self whose existence is dependent upon its interaction with and appearance to others.

Specific identity markers worn by women in villages in the West Bank indicate their social standing. For example, a woman may wear a *mandīl*, or headcovering, as a significant indication of her religiosity or modesty. A bride wears her gold at her engagement and wedding; she is "dressed" by her groom on both occasions in the presence of other women who sing and dance throughout. The gold jewelry acts as a key symbol of the bride's changed (and improved) status. Although most married women wear their gold jewelry only on special occasions, they wear wedding rings at all times. A photo of Hilma Granqvist, the Finnish anthropologist who lived in Artas from 1925 to 1931, shows her dressed as an Artasi (a villager from Artas) bride, an outward symbol of her status as an accepted Artasi woman (figure 1.1).[2]

Older peasant women still often wear the hand-embroidered *thōb*, or long dress, signifying their status as established village women. The *thōb* has historically reflected whether a woman was "a townswoman, villager or bedouin, and varied in more detailed ways according to the region, village or tribe to which she belonged" (Weir 1989: 76; Rajab 1989). Festive occasions have been traditional places for a woman to wear her most elaborate and distinctive *thōb* (Weir 1989: 76). Weir argues that central and southern Palestine can be divided into three areas, characterized by whether the primary garments worn by women are white, mid to dark blue, or white or black (1989: 88). Weir further describes the embroidery that decorates the dresses:

> Women have a strong sense of village identity and pride which is expressed in specific designs and motifs, and in an aesthetic idiom. The women of each village say they embroidered one way rather than another because 'that was our custom (sibrna)', or 'because it looks better that way.' (1989: 104)

Figure 1.1.   Dr. Hilma Granqvist dressed for a wedding in the village of Artas (PEF/P/GRAN/MI/10). Reproduced by the permission of The Palestine Exploration Fund, London.

Married women of childbearing age have historically worn the most lavish embroidery; it was considered shameful (*'aib*) for an unmarried or menopausal woman to wear such decoration (Weir 1989: 105).

Young women in Artas (and most women in urban areas in the Palestinian West Bank) now generally refuse to wear the traditional *thōb*, preferring to buy their clothing at trendy shops in Bethlehem. Indeed, as villagers explained to me, the clothes that cover the body of a young woman in Artas have in many cases circulated between Palestinians and Israelis. The clothes that Palestinian women sew in small factories throughout the West Bank are often subcontracted by Israeli shop owners who attach their labels to the clothing and then sell it to Palestinian shop owners.[3] As in North America, it is the label that gives the piece of clothing some of its status and determines its worth. This process virtually assures that some young Palestinian and Israeli women are wearing identically designed and sewn clothing. To some Palestinian women, knowing that they are probably dressed identically to some Israeli women is unsettling, as their externalized selves would then be indistinguishable from Israeli women's externalized selves. A neighbor of mine, for example, unabashedly wore Israeli and American-label clothes and was often criticized by her neighbors for it. Complicating matters was the fact that her clothes were bought with money her husband earned working as a foreman on an Israeli construction site. Although she also earned a salary as a teacher, this fact was generally overlooked. Wearing foreign-label clothes edges young women toward dangerous moral behavior: Although they buy the foreign label clothes that are modest now, the possibility that they may later choose more risqué styles (and, eventually, lifestyles) is omnipresent.

Yet young women and men view new clothes as a precious commodity. They are highly sought after and desired objects. If clothes are one's externalized self, then new clothes indicate a wealthy and successful life. Old clothes are often stigmatized as reflections of poverty and a lack of success; indeed, Maysa, mother of my host family in the village, would often refuse to go out if she felt she did not have nice clothes to wear, commenting that it was *'aib*, shameful, for herself and her husband Nidal.[4] One day Maysa commented to me that she could not understand how a young relative of hers was unhappy, as she had a closet full of new clothes—and what else could a newlywed want?

In contrast to young people's desires for the latest fashions, Yassir Arafat and other Palestinian nationalists have often used traditional sartorial markers of peasant social status. Arafat wears the *kufiya*, or headscarf, most commonly worn by village men. He may do so to demonstrate his solidarity with villagers and to demonstrate publicly that, at least symbolically, he is one of them.[5] During the first intifada, some young women in the West Bank wore "flag dresses," dresses made from cheap synthetic fabrics that resemble the traditional *thōb*, in order "to represent themselves as standard bearers of the future nation" (Sherwell 1996: 301). Pictures of young women wearing beautifully embroidered *thōbs* are published by the Palestinian National Council (PNC) and distributed widely throughout the West Bank and, indeed, the Palestinian diaspora.

In the Artas Folklore Center, Mr. Musa Sanad (the Director) has hung many of the PNC's photographs. He also asked his young female relatives to dress in *thōbs* and pose for pictures for the center, but they adamantly refused to wear, as they put it, "their grandmothers' clothing". Nonetheless, on the front page of the pamphlet Mr. Sanad published about the center and its activities is a picture of a young woman dressed in a traditional *thōb* (figure 1.2), while on the back page of the pamphlet appeared advertisements for contemporary clothes for men, women, and children (figure 1.3). While the

Figure 1.2.   Artas Folklore Center brochure, front page.

Figure 1.3.   Artas Folklore Center brochure, back page.

former picture shows a young Palestinian woman dressed in traditional clothing, items that have historically signified her social and, indeed, political, status, the latter reflects a new image for young people, but one that retains a
sense of the importance of clothing as an external signifier.

Wearing a jinn, like wearing clothing and other identity markers, is an externalized expression of the status of a woman's social self—which, depending on the nature of the experience of possession, may be temporarily eclipsed,
subsumed by the presence of the jinn, or troubled by the jinn's influence. Pos-

session by the jinn, like old or foreign clothes or a bride's jewelry, may be discussed by villagers who do not know the possessed woman personally but realize the jinn's symbolic and public importance. As clothes and jewelry signify certain common points of reference and experience for most villagers (e.g., wealth or poverty or marital status), so jinn stories rely on shared themes in villagers' daily lives and experiences. If the villagers know the possessed person personally, they may also understand possession experiences as evidence of specific problems or possible moral transgressions. Yet when a jinn story is told and retold, it gains a progressively wider social significance.

Unlike the gold jewelry given to a bride at her wedding that is often mercilessly evaluated by other women in daily conversation about its worth, stories of the jinn speak to issues that are, in the course of normal conversation, rarely directly addressed. Some stories of the jinn were told to me with significant elaboration, while others drew heavily on villagers' implicit knowledge of their social world. This knowledge, according to Boddy (1989: 4) "goes without saying." In what follows here I interpret these stories according to the understandings I gained about villagers' social world.

THE JINN AS DISCOURSE

As jinn stories are told and retold, they exist in both a subjugated (cf. Foucault 1980) and dialectical relationship to the dominant cultural discourses on Islam, honor, family unity, and Palestinian nationalism. These dominant discourses demand both adherence and support in varying degrees from individuals who would risk their social standing in the village or, indeed, their personal safety, if they voiced explicitly dissenting sentiments.[6] Jinn stories subtly direct their listeners to experiences, opinions, and emotions that would otherwise, in all likelihood, be left unsaid for fear of a range of possible reprisals; jinn stories are thus easy to miss. Yet dominant discourses are never wholly successful in suppressing people's beliefs, thoughts, and experiences, although they may significantly quiet and/or circumscribe them to being voiced through subordinate discourses located in particular social spaces (e.g., Abu-Lughod 1986, Boddy 1989, Ong 1987). Jinn narratives are a subtle means for women and men to negotiate social relationships, to indicate forces and/or people they find oppressive or difficult to deal with, and to grapple with the power and control of tradition, personal circumstance, patriarchy, and occupation.

The term *discourse* in anthropological studies may refer to a range of cultural productions, including texts, performances, and speech events (see Bowen 1993: 8–9). Jinn stories are dealt with here as primarily speech events, but with an ear that is ever attuned to their relationship to the more powerful

discourses of all kinds in village society. As a subjugated discourse, jinn stories exist in a power-laden, critical, and challenging relationship to the more
powerful discourses that are typically publicly upheld and defended as "natural" or "right." Jinn stories contain within them potentially explosive and revealing sentiments, critiques, and understandings of village life, but in a way
that does not directly confront or undermine the power or truth claims of the
dominant discourses. Indeed, the jinn discourse is integral to the dominant
ones by providing a safe outlet for villagers' social critiques, while allowing
for both the perpetuation of the stories and the assurance of the integrity of
the women and men who espouse them.

Stories of the jinn have often been relegated to the realm of folk tales or
fantasy. In their study of Palestinian Arab folktales, Muhawi and Kanaana
note that numerous types of folk narratives are common among Palestinians:
folktales, illustrating proverbs, tales of rare events, re-creations of past oc-
currences, animal fables, jinn tales, saints' legends, myths, and memorates
(1989: 3). They note that only folktales among these narrative forms require
a special setting, linguistic style, and "narrative attitude" (1989:5). The others are related spontaneously when they are appropriate to the conversation
taking place. Further, these other narrative forms, including jinn tales, "are
rarely told for their own sake, as folktales are, but are usually used to illus-
trate a point, offer subtle recommendation concerning behavior, or volunteer
a different perspective on a subject" (Muhawi and Kanaana 1989: 3–4).
Indeed.

Jinn stories are recognized as distinct from folktales by villagers in Artas,
as Muhawi and Kanaana note, although the line between the two may in particular instances become blurred, particularly when a jinn story becomes very
well known, refers to an anonymous person, and comes to be told in a highly
stylized manner. As discussed in the next chapter, I recorded one jinn story
that was told to me in a nearly identical manner to one recorded in the 1920s
by Mary Crowfoot and Louise Baldensperger (published by Barghouthi
1987). This story is an exception to the other jinn stories I gathered; I include
it to suggest that jinn stories today are not a wholly new cultural practice. Yet
village elders may not recognize many of today's jinn stories as typical jinn
stories in Artas, although some stories do seem to display a certain historical
continuity with jinn stories of the past. Contrary to folktales, most jinn stories
I heard would not stand alone: The stories are typically condensed, referen-
tial, and lack meaning without significant social context.

While Muhawi and Kanaana do not expound on the meanings inherent in
jinn stories, they point to the nature of jinn stories as speech events—as
discourse—rather than the physicality or embodiment of the possession experience itself. Although I witnessed treatment sessions and spoke with those
who considered themselves to be bothered or, in a sense, "haunted" on an on-

who considered themselves to be bothered or, in a sense, "haunted" on an on-going basis by the jinn, I never saw a case of full-fledged bodily possession (such as a case including a trance). This does not mean that bodily experiences of possession do not occur; villagers told me that they do, but that such events are relatively uncommon. It is thus in the telling and retelling of women's and men's stories of the jinn that I have looked for meaning (cf. Badone 1989, Mattingly 1998).

Stories that are heard and repeated by villagers are typically not told as evidence of an individual's fantasy; indeed, the individual who had the experience with the jinn may be unknown to either the teller of the tale or his/her listeners, making it difficult to judge such matters. To focus on the "truth" of such matters as jinn stories is to miss the point that the stories are relevant for what they say about villagers' social circumstances rather than personal idiosyncrasies.

Jinn stories straddle a number of areas of inquiry: the political use of narrative (e.g., Crain 1991; Jameson 1981); the politics of coexisting, unequal discourses (e.g., Lambek 1993); and the roles of spirits and religious belief in daily life (e.g., Mageo and Howard 1996). They probe the boundaries of power, resistance, religious experience, family constitution, and gender roles, as well as the politics of occupation, love, honor, and pride. The stories cannot be analyzed in isolation from the political economy and moral world that inform them. But they also cannot be reduced to only those circumstances, lest we risk denying the veracity of beliefs in the spirits themselves. In this book I look at jinn stories as part of a subjugated discourse used primarily by young and middle-aged Artasis, and one which is relatively common, politically current, and extraordinarily malleable.

SOCIAL GEOGRAPHY

The largely implicit principles and logic of what I have termed *social geography* are key referents for understanding jinn stories and their meanings for the women and men who tell and hear them. The concept of social geography recognizes the central role of geographical proximity in the creation of women's most central and meaningful social relationships, or, to paraphrase my informants, the "kind of family that matters."

Looking closely at the experience of "closeness" and how it is created and fostered is the starting point for understanding how social geography works. The word for "close"—*qarīb*—has two meanings in everyday usage: first, a sense of physical or geographical proximity, and second, a sense of someone who is "closely," or, genealogically, related (cf. Moors 1995: 87-91). Often, the two senses of the word coincide, as when an immediate family member

lives nearby. Indeed, many members of any one *ḥamūla*, an extended, patrilineal family, often live near one another in the village and are at once both
neighbors and genealogical relatives. Each neighborhood, or *ḥāra*, is tightly
knit, intimately familiar with the comings and goings of its members, and
well aware of the presence of a stranger. Young women in particular may be
completely unfamiliar with parts of the village less than half a kilometer away
from their own, since they have little reason to visit those who live there. Yet
a man may be described as an *"ibn balad,"* or son of the village,[7] if he is recognized as being from the village but the speaker has forgotten his name. This
phrase emphasizes both their proximity to one another and a potential genealogical link.

Most villagers' "mental map" of the village is a map of the locations of the
homes of each *ḥamūla* in the various neighborhoods of the village. While a
family from one *ḥamūla* may purchase a home in a different *ḥamūla's* neighborhood, the range of possible ties among families is such that a genealogical
link can generally be found, through the use of an often distant past and complex genealogical tracing (cf. Antoun 1972: 134). In Artas, a family tie can
almost always be "found" to link any two individuals. After all, the history of
the village and of intermarriage among the various families is long, as are
many elderly villagers' memories.

When village residents are *qarīb*[8] but not *qarīb*—kin but not close by, or
close by but not genealogically related—a challenge is posed to the generally
accepted idea that kin are those whom one should know well, or, conversely,
that a neighbor of many years is not kin. When the two meanings of *qarīb* are
considered separately, it clearly emerges that what is often most important for
women's daily lives is physical closeness and carefully fostered familiarity,
without which a blood tie lacks meaning. Writing of a neighborhood street in
a community in Lebanon, Joseph argues:

> Intense and deep relations developed among the street women. They relied on
> one another continually for services, using one another's children to run errands
> and do housework, borrowing money from one another, and depending on one
> another for emotional and moral support. There is a saying in Arabic, 'The
> neighbor who is near is better than the brother who is far away.' (1978: 548)

These experiences and this saying are common in Artas as well.

The "kind of family that matters" for many women is thus shaped by a
sense of friendship created, in large part, through the circumstances of being
physically close to one another. This particular kind of family is developed
and maintained through social geography, a concept that recognizes that
physical proximity and women's individual preferences allow for the development of reciprocal relationships and friendships that are important to the
workings of women's daily lives. It is geographical proximity that creates the

most immediate possibility for an ethic of neighborliness—the practice of reciprocity between women who live close to one another based upon their shared friendship—and a sense of emotionally informed family that is both powerful and long-lasting.

The enactment of this ethic of neighborliness includes relying on one another for help with housework or to make up a deficit of food or goods. Neighbors may turn to one another for emotional support or advice. They may orchestrate the marriages of their children, thereby solidifying "closeness" and creating genealogical ties where there may have been none (or relatively weak links) before. Or, neighbors may alert one another to potential spouses for their children in different parts of the village. Of course, these relations can also be manipulated, so that overusing one's neighbor's resources can be seen as a kind of social condemnation of some aspect of her behavior. Yet what is most important here is that these relations are chosen by the neighboring women and fostered according to their individual preferences, and that these relations are of central importance to women's lives.

Although there are many genealogical terms for specific family relationships and distinct words for friends and neighbors, in practice these relations may be indistinguishable. As H. Geertz points out, in Morocco speech distinctions are made between "what we would call 'kinsman' and what we would consider 'non-kin' on essentially biogenetic grounds; the operative, everyday, acted-upon premises do not rely on sharp and simple distinctions among family, friend, and patron" (1979: 315). The bonds of friendship are marked by the "diffuse, enduring solidarity" typical of kinship bonds (Schneider 1980). In spite of the importance of friendship as an analytical category, it is often marginalized by scholars, who may minimize such relationships as "fictive kinship" or ignore them altogether (Weston 1995: 94).

Why does friendship appear as a "signifier of stability" (Weston 1995) in relationships? Under what kind of historical circumstances has this notion evolved? For Artasi villagers, the ready existence of a history of ties which can be found to link almost any two neighbors, coupled with the pressure of emigration from the village and the fact that many families are forcibly divided because of Israeli restrictions on who was allowed to return to the West Bank after the 1967 occupation, make enduring physical presence as well as individual preference key factors in creating key social ties. Indeed, if almost anyone can be considered kin (albeit to varying degrees) and, simultaneously, the threat of departure from the village is seen as always imminent, the people who matter most are those upon whom one can rely and those whom one cares about.[9]

Thus women carefully choose their friendships in the *hāra* and through those friendships create the grounds for meaningful and long-lasting ties. Closely located and well-liked neighbors are felt to be "closer" than more directly related but disliked relatives who may live in the same degree of proximity. For example, a female neighbor of mine in the village lived just a few houses away from her father and stepbrothers, but she had no contact with them. Having a genealogical link and living in close proximity is not enough to create a sense of closeness or community—or "the kind of family that matters"—among women. Two women I knew who were married to two brothers, for example, lived on different floors of the same extended family household but rarely spoke; indeed, one did not attend the other's son's wedding.

Further, since in Artas so many kin live far from the village—unable to return due to Israeli restrictions and consequently unknown to the younger generation—many kin are strangers because they are long-term residents of the diaspora.[10] For young people in particular, these relatives may be virtually unknown or known only from occasional visits to the village. In these cases, it is often difficult for young people to reconcile their expectations to feel "close" to family members with their lived experiences of meeting those long-distance relatives only rarely and feeling that they are strangers. As we will see, this paradox informs a specific strand of stories of the jinn.

All this is not to claim that the relations between neighbors always, or even in most cases, supersede those between genealogically-reckoned relatives. Rather, the emphasis here is that it is possible that they *could* and sometimes do, and that neighborly relationships depend on the recognition of an individual woman's choice, instead of a mechanical or purely self-interested fulfillment of kinship roles or neighborly duties. Indeed, relations between extended family members may be very close. In such cases they are often characterized by women as being a relation of sisters—the epitome of a close relationship—no matter the actual link. Yet good relations are also often seen as fortuitous—it is a happy coincidence to like one's relatives (just as it is equally fortuitous to like one's neighbors). Extended family members who do not live near one another may get to know each other over the years if they invest time visiting one another, and women may choose to foster those friendships over other more conveniently located ones.

Jinn stories illuminate aspects of the logic of social geography that are typically felt more than expressed, experienced rather than analyzed. A focus on social geography thus leads to examining the nature of social relations among those forcibly separated by distance and those unwillingly brought together, including the relations of villagers to family members in the diaspora, or Palestinian men to their Israeli prison guards. Jinn stories reflect on the complexity of these relationships, articulate their strains, and at times suggest what may seem unthinkable, or, at least, quite unexpected. Together, the concept and practices of social geography and stories of the jinn create a complex and rich picture of villagers' relationships to one another, to their family members in the Palestinian diaspora, and to their Jewish neighbors—a picture that is at times surprising and always revealing.

METHODOLOGY

I had originally come to Artās to study changing kinship relations as a follow-up of the work of Finnish anthropologist Hilma Granqvist in Artas in the 1920s.[11] When I heard my first jinn story, however, I quickly made the decision to follow this lead. But my initial plan was not entirely dropped: notions of kinship were an obvious key to understanding the jinn narratives, as were numerous other dimensions of social relations.

Stories of the jinn were told to me in a variety of contexts, sometimes due to my prompting and at other times because they simply came up in conversation. They were whispered to me in semiprivate spaces or told to me in large, mixed-group settings. Some villagers refused to tell me their own stories of possession (often knowing that I had heard about their experiences from others), while others described in detail their ordeals. There is no formula for predicting when a jinn story might be mentioned or told in detail and by whom; I do believe, however, that the most complex and sensitive of the stories were told only among close friends and family and not in front of those of the opposite gender.

It is difficult to estimate with any accuracy the number of women who consider themselves to be or to have been afflicted by the jinn. I did not carry out a survey of village-wide beliefs in the jinn; the family with whom I lived initially strongly encouraged me to remain in our neighborhood for the sake of my reputation (and theirs), and later in my fieldwork, I found that I felt most comfortable in our *hāra*. As a rough estimate, I would suggest that perhaps one in every ten women narrated to me her own jinn story, while nearly every woman I asked about the jinn was able to tell me of someone's experience with the spirits. Yet I am not overly concerned here with presenting a statistical account of experiences with the jinn; this would present a misleading picture in many respects, even if the necessary data were available. Perhaps most problematically, statistical analysis could suggest that jinn episodes happen at a constant or fixed rate, while my impression is that jinn episodes seem highly variable in their rate of occurrence. I do know that jinn stories are of interest to all who hear about them, incorporate knowledge of them into their daily lives, and then proceed to tell the stories to others. It would be difficult to capture this fluid process in a statistic.

It is interesting to note, however, that in a 1992 survey of 2,500 Palestinian households in Gaza, the West Bank, and Arab Jerusalem (referred to hereafter as the 1992 FAFO survey), 12 percent of respondents who experienced illness contacted traditional healers, 89 percent contacted a physician, 22 percent contacted a nurse/pharmacist, and 14 percent treated themselves. These figures suggest that many Palestinians view these options as possible to pursue simultaneously (these figures come to a total of 137 percent) and not exclusively (Giacaman, Stoltenberg, and Weiseth 1994: 112). I argue that if 12 percent of respondents were willing to admit to an unknown surveyor that they contacted traditional healers, a matter often thought of by villagers as both private and sensitive, the actual percentage is in all likelihood higher. As some kinds of illness experiences are believed to be caused by a jinn and these illnesses are best treated by "traditional healers," we may speculate that this statistic may be suggestive of beliefs in the jinn and their possible physical effects, albeit not exclusively.

At times, my interest in jinn narratives led me outside of Artas. With the help of my research assistant, a young man from the house next door, I traveled to Bethlehem, Hebron, and Nablus to talk to local experts on the jinn. I found these individuals with the help of Artasis who had used their services for curing jinn troubles in the past. Although my research assistant could not accompany me to Amman, Jordan, I also traveled there to stay with his family members after meeting them in Artas.

While I have drawn my data and conclusions primarily from my months of observation, informal and formal interviews, and countless casual conversations, I have also included here an analysis of a serialized jinn story related anonymously as an autobiography in the Palestinian magazine *Fosta*[12] (see chapter 5), a relatively cheap, popular, and sensationalist magazine. By including this story, which discusses a young man's detailed adventures with a female jinn, or jinnia, the discussion of jinn stories and social geography as meaningful to all Artasis, but particularly for young men, is deepened. Further, through this analysis both the shared and divergent ways in which men and women experience and tell stories of the jinn are made clear. My interpretation of this story is based on a number of directed discussions with young Artasis and Muslim students at nearby Bethlehem University about the story's content and meaning for them.

There is an extensive popular literary jinn genre in Arabic; these books are easily found in street corner newsstands and all kinds of bookstores in Cairo, Damascus, and Amman (and I would guess elsewhere in the Middle East, but my own observations are limited to these cities). A discussion of these texts is beyond the scope of this ethnography precisely because this material was not owned or read by anyone I knew in Artas. Yet the magazine *Fosta* was known and discussed by a number of my younger friends in Artas, making it a meaningful source of thought and reflection for them and thus for me as well.[13] An in-depth examination of the Qu'ranic verses and other Islamic textually based teachings about the jinn is also outside the scope of the analysis here, as no one I interviewed referred to these text sources beyond stating that the jinn themselves are legitimate Islamic beliefs since they are known to be mentioned in the Qu'ran.

IDENTITY

At the time of my fieldwork cautious optimism was shared by many Artasis about the possibility of peace, or, at least, better times, which I discuss later in this chapter. This sense of possibility framed my fieldwork in important ways; indeed, this particular time period was a window of opportunity for me to participate in villagers' daily lives as, at the least, a potential friend. A history of female researchers in the village—including those women well-known to readers of older literature on Palestine, including the daughter of French missionaries, Louise Baldensperger, and Finnish anthropologist Hilma Granqvist; as well as lesser known but still remembered women, such as the American Jewish researcher Judith Blanc—further framed my presence in Artas in important ways and shaped my research questions. Unable to claim a genealogy based on kinship ties, I was taught by the villagers that I was part of a genealogy of foreign female researchers in Artas with whom they had many previous connections; these connections to my "foremothers" were important precipitating links to me (see Rothenberg 1999a for this discussion).

Discussions of the politics of identity in fieldwork (e.g., Altorki and El-Solh 1988; Kulick and Wilson 1995; Wolf 1996) and the representation of the anthropologist in the ethnography (Behar and Gordon 1995; Clifford and Marcus 1986; Marcus and Fischer 1986) are now ubiquitous in many anthropological circles. As this book is about social relations and religious belief in Artas, this area seems to me to be the best place to start in a discussion of my identity during my fieldwork and within this text, as well. In the eyes of Israeli law, my Jewish identity while in the field was highly suspect: my mother is a Jewish convert who did not undergo the Orthodox Jewish conversion process, but rather a Reform Jewish one. My father's family is Jewish, while my mother's parents were Lutheran Swedes. As Jewish identity is considered to be passed down only through the mother (not the father and, indeed, only when the mother is from an orthodox family), I was not considered legally Jewish in Israel, although I had been raised in a liberal Jewish home. I used this ambiguity in my Jewish status while doing my fieldwork. In some instances, I shared with close friends the details of my mixed family heritage, while preferring my legally correct if not entirely forthcoming answer when responding to questions about my religion from those whom I did not know well. This latter option was not just an avenue for maintaining my privacy. The family with whom I lived in Artas felt, and I agreed, that I should be careful with this information. As far as social relations go, through my "close" family relations (sibling, aunts, uncles, and first cousins) I am related to Catholics, Lutherans, Reform Jews, Orthodox Jews, and Muslims. I am also an American who has lived in Canada for nearly ten years. I have often felt a sense of liminality when it comes to identifying myself with exclusive social categories.

I have been fascinated with the Palestinians since I was an undergraduate: I wrote my undergraduate honor's thesis on Palestinian women's organizations, worked for a peace organization in Israel, and studied Arabic for many years. Often villagers joked with me that if I were an Israeli spy my Arabic would have been far better, a comment on both the pervasive practices of Israeli surveillance as well as my pronounced accent. I am still working out what my identity meant to villagers, to their sense of my own and their own power, and to my fieldwork experience: this process is ongoing. Yet I stand firmly by my original perception that the history of female researchers in Artas was central to framing my presence and purpose in Artas. Villagers located me repeatedly within this genealogy. To overlook this fact or minimize it with respect to my American Jewish identity would serve only to ignore villagers', and especially women's, voices.

The majority of villagers with whom I spent my days were gracious, welcoming, and protective, sometimes to the point that I believe they spared me some of their analyses of the Israeli-Palestinian conflict, opinions of Americans, and ideas about Jews. A few people were openly hostile to my presence, but these individuals were a small minority. Of course, in certain respects this lack of open sharing of sentiments was a drawback, limiting the information I was able to gain. In other respects, however, this withholding was a symbol of how neighbors in close proximity treat one another in the hopes of creating long-lasting ties. In short, I decided to look at this treatment in the only way an anthropologist can: as data.

In December 2000, more than four years after I returned to Toronto from Artas, 'Adil (a pseudonym for the young man who worked as my research assistant and is the son of one of my closest neighbors in the village) came to live with me, my husband, and children for six months. We assisted him with his Canadian Landed Immigrant application, and he has just recently received his landing papers. I have found it both hilarious and wonderful to be at my home in Toronto, answer the phone, and hear my beloved neighbor's voice as clearly as if she were still next door saying, *ya Celia, ya habla!* (Celia, you fool!), as she did in greeting me in Artas as part of a long-standing joke between us (the details of which I will spare my readers, but I will say it had to do with me, with her, and my attempts to bake bread in a *ṭābūn*, an outdoor oven).

'Adil's distance from his family is both symbolically and physically meaningful, and it will have significant consequences for both him and the relatives he has left behind. The fact that I have facilitated his departure is somewhat troubling to me. Yet it was his dream to come to live in Canada and eventually to bring here as many members of his family as wish to emigrate. He will now have the possibility of creating an entirely new network of close relationships, while in all likelihood he has by his decision foregone many other kinds of networks. As will become clear in the discussion of social geography in the pages to follow, personal preference is a central factor in creating an individual's most meaningful ties. My young friend has, for the time being, expressed his preference. (I should point out that he will not find stories of the jinn here in Canada, and that this, too, has particular consequences for the Palestinian immigrants who live in Toronto; see Gibb and Rothenberg 2000.) Yet without a doubt his presence in Toronto has helped me remain in touch with current developments in Artas and to continue to think about and discuss with him my fieldwork material, an opportunity for which I am deeply grateful.

ARTAS

Artasis number approximately 3,000, with an additional 3,000 villagers living outside the West Bank in the Palestinian diaspora, according to Musa Sanad, the village historian who is arguably the man most knowledgeable about the history and current circumstances of the village.[14] In some respects, Artasis are practically suburbanites to nearby Bethlehem and, although slightly further away, to Jerusalem.[15] One of three or four cars in service on a given day leaves Artas each hour packed with women and children heading for Bethlehem's main square just two miles down the road, where Artasi women do most of their shopping. Young women in particular will buy chic, modest (arms and legs covered) clothing, the latest music tapes from Egypt and Jordan, costume jewelry, nail polish, and makeup. Married women will typically do the family's grocery shopping there, returning to Artas with large quantities of fresh vegetables and fruit, meat, cooking oil, rice, and other necessities.

Over the years a number of villagers have moved to Bethlehem, and Artasi villagers may visit these relatives occasionally. It is rare for villagers to socialize extensively with Christians in Bethlehem, although many men maintain working or business relations with them. From Bethlehem cars leave for Jerusalem three or four times an hour, filled with men going to work and women going to visit family, make special shopping trips, or travel to a hospital or office. A few older women from Artas sell vegetables or other produce they have cultivated in Jerusalem and other nearby cities.

Artas is part of the Bethlehem district (an area encompassing Bethlehem and its surrounding villages), which, at the time of my fieldwork, came under semiautonomous Palestinian control. The Bethlehem district is considered to be in the highlands, bordered on the west by the coastal plains of Israel and on the east by the Jordan valley. Artas rises upward on the southern slopes of Jabal Zahir (Mount Zahir) and spreads down into the valley; the village faces Jabal Abu Zaid in the south. It is possible to enter Artas from the north by the paved road that links it directly with Bethlehem. From the west, Artas can be reached by following the main road that runs from Jerusalem, past Bethlehem, and ultimately to Hebron; between Bethlehem and Hebron, this road passes a small turn-off, which leads to Solomon's Pools and into Artas.

Villagers described to me how, before the first intifada broke out in 1987, Solomon's Pools were once a peaceful picnic spot for both Israelis and Palestinians. These pools furnished Jerusalem with its water supply for centuries, but today two of the three pools are filled with stagnant water and garbage. One pool, thanks to the nearly single-handed efforts of Mr. Sanad, was cleaned during my fieldwork and served as the site of the first Palestinian Folkore Festival—the first large-scale, public celebration of Palestinian culture since well before the start of the 1987 intifada. Ten minutes further down the road from Solomon's Pools lies the southern edge of Artas.

The convent in Artas' valley (Convent of the Nuns of the Closed Paradise), while a lesser-known attraction than Solomon's Pools, is popular with historically-minded Christian tourists and is a striking part of the village landscape. The nuns and their hired workers (from Artas and other villages in the area) cultivate a large portion of the land in the valley. Yet villagers and the nuns have little sustained social contact. Villagers may buy eggs, vegetables, or fruits from the nuns occasionally, or ask the nuns to administer shots or medicines. The nuns do not proselytize among the villagers, nor do they attend village social events. Most villagers and the nuns describe their relations with one another as good, if socially distant. This sense of social distance with neighbors in close proximity is not new. In 1975, a team of three researchers carried out a study of "patterns of socialization in an Arab village [Artas]" (Antonovsky, Meari, and Blanc 1975); they, too, noted that "relations between village and convent are generally civil but minimal" (1975: 7). This social fact is interesting in light of the emphasis here on social geography. Clearly, very close proximity does not insure or predict a close relationship.

Artas is home to a mosque and a kindergarten; there is also a spring that is still used for washing clothes. The village has sex-segregated schools for girls and boys (providing at the time of my fieldwork education until the ninth and eleventh grades, respectively). Pupils who wished to complete high school and the high school certificate exams (*tawjihi*), had to commute to Bethlehem, a factor which contributed to girls' high dropout rate in particular. A doctor sees patients twice a month in a one-room structure located along the road from Bethlehem, although many Artas residents go to the hospital in Bethlehem or to medical centers in Jerusalem when they need to see specialists or when they experience a medical emergency. There are a few small shops scattered throughout the village, selling primarily sweets, household cleaning items, and a small assortment of convenience goods.

Many men in Artas find work building Israeli settlements in Israel and the West Bank; unfortunately, I cannot offer statistics for Artasi men's employment with certainty, as I did not go from household to household beyond my neighborhood. However, based on the 1992 FAFO survey, approximately 90 percent of the labor force in the occupied territories was male; approximately 26 percent of this labor force worked in Israel and 45 percent in the West Bank. Forty-five percent of residents in the occupied territories employed in Israel worked in construction; approximately 10 percent of employed persons who resided in the occupied territories worked in the occupied territories in construction (Ovensen 1994: 204-5). In my neighborhood, many men from one extended household in particular worked on Israeli construction sites. Indeed, one of these men was a foreman and was consequently able to employ a number of his close male relations. Other jobs held by men in the neighborhood included those of schoolteacher, gardener, and police officer.

Neighborhoods often seem to extend as much vertically as horizontally in Artas, because the village sits on a relatively steep slope. Newer houses are made of cement. New homes of relatively wealthy residents have cement-poured walls lined with white stone. Older homes were built from stones pulled from the surrounding rocky mountainsides. Many of these older homes provide foundations for additions; there are an increasing number of two or three-story structures around the village. Additions have reached the point of blocking many villagers' views of the valley and hillside, in spite of the fact that the houses are built on a steep slope. During my fieldwork many families built additional stories on their older homes, and since my departure I have been told of numerous more such additions.

On the opposite side of Jabal Zahir sprawls one of the West Bank's largest refugee camps, Deheisha.[16] Many villagers describe the refugees as essentially different from long-established village families in terms of both character and morals, but hostility between the two groups is slowly diminishing as villagers and Deheisha residents buy land and build houses on Deheisha's edge. Indeed, the space between Artas and Deheisha is closing. It remains to be seen how the increasing physical proximity of the two will affect future social relations.

Artas is known for its Folklore Center, established and run by Musa Sanad. A description of the center now available on the World Wide Web reads:

> The Artas Folklore Center was founded in 1993 with the aim of preserving traditional Palestinian heritage. It is the first project of its kind, a specialized center functioning in a historical building, located in the natural setting of a Palestinian village. It participates actively in festivals and organizes its own festivals. The center includes a small museum housing a photographic record of traditional

Palestinian life. It organizes training courses for women and girls (sewing, agri-
culture and flower arranging). It also organizes a Day for Palestinian
Popular Heritage celebrations. (http://www.bethlehem-city.org/The_District/b_
Artas_list.htm)

Since my fieldwork the center has changed its location in the village. When I
was there it was a modestly furnished place, with a few posters, photographs,
and postcards on its walls, and a few pieces of furniture (a desk, chair, and
table). I understand the center has grown in size considerably since my departure and now has a computer and phone.

Mr. Sanad's dedication to preserving the culture and history of
Artas is impressive. At the outset of my fieldwork, professors at both Bir Zeit
University and Bethlehem University referred me to him. Upon meeting Mr.
Sanad and explaining to him my hopes to pursue research that would follow-
up aspects of Granqvist's work in Artas, he immediately committed himself
to my aid, arranged for me to live in the village, shared some of his data about
village life with me, and regularly checked on my progress.

Mr. Sanad's generous services have been used by many researchers—
Palestinian and non-Palestinian—who have furthered their own academic ca-
reers with little thought to his own aspirations. I fear that this is another genealogy in which I also find myself. An elementary school village math teacher, Mr.
Sanad has not had access to or invitations from the halls of higher education and
the academy, although he has been in the position of holding the key for others
to enter them. I know he has wished that this were not the case, and that he, too,
could find a way to publish his materials and be recognized as the expert that he
is. When I returned to Toronto after my fieldwork, I sent him bound photocopies
of all of Granqvist's books. I sent him my thesis when I finished it, and I will
send him a copy of this book upon its publication. I credit him and his work in
my text where I have used, with his permission, his data about marriages (see the
appendix); he shared these data with me with his usual supreme generosity. I
wish I could do more to enable him to realize his own ambitions. Mr. Sanad
strongly encouraged me to follow my interests in jinn stories, recognizing them
as important products of a rich cultural knowledge and heritage. This book represents what I can do for him here. I hope this book will bring him wider, much
deserved recognition, though I alone am responsible for its faults.

CAUGHT IN THE MIDDLE
OF FOUR MOUNTAINS

Artasis describe the history of their village as a story of one place caught in
the middle of four mountains, a metaphor for their feelings of entrapment by
the series of occupiers—the Ottomans (1516–1917), British (1917–1948), Jor-

danians (1948–1967), and Israelis (1967 to the present, in varying degrees)—who have come to the West Bank. In the same way that mountains are immovable, so, too, have the occupations seemed to linger. During my fieldwork, the Palestinian Authority assumed control of civil matters in parts of the West Bank (including the area containing Artas). Yet the history of occupations has made many villagers skeptical and pessimistic about what will come next, either from their own government or from a new (or old) foreign power.

The window of time during which I conducted my fieldwork allowed me to focus on villagers' perceptions and practices of social relations and their stories of the jinn, not to the exclusion of experiences of foreign domination, but as complement to them. The Declaration of Principles (DOP), or, Oslo Accords, signed on September 13, 1993 by Yassir Arafat and Yitzhak Rabin, raised the hopes of ending the intifada that had begun in 1987, opening a new and promising chapter in Israeli-Palestinian relations, and allowing for Palestinian self-rule. The DOP provided a framework for the creation of a Palestinian self-governing authority for a transitional period that would last for not more than five years. In May 1994 the Agreement on the Gaza Strip and Jericho Area (the Cairo agreement) and in August 1994 the Agreement on Preparatory Transfer of Powers and Responsibilities were also agreed upon (see Shehadeh 1995 for a brief overview of these agreements).

"Oslo II," or the Interim Agreement, was signed in late September 1995, a few months after I arrived in Artas. I described in my field notes how I sat with numerous members of my host family watching Shimon Peres and Yassir Arafat on television as they signed a plan for increasing autonomy in parts of the West Bank. It was an optimistic time. The West Bank was divided into three zones by Oslo II: Zone A included areas in the West Bank which were completely under Palestinian autonomy; Zone B was under shared Israeli and Palestinian control, whereby Israel retained control of security matters and the Palestinians exercised autonomous civil rule; and Zone C was under Israeli control (this zone included Israeli settlements, army bases, and military zones). Artas was located in Zone B, which included approximately 450 Palestinian villages and most rural areas (see map on page ii).

Israeli Prime Minister Yitzhak Rabin was assassinated by an Israeli Jew after he spoke at a massive peace rally inside Israel on November 4, 1995. I vividly remember learning the news of Rabin's death: I had come downstairs to help Maysa, the mother of the family, prepare the children for school. She said simply that Rabin was dead and that responsibility for his death would surely fall on the heads of Palestinians. The implications were sickening: if a Palestinian had killed Rabin there would be a terrible price to pay. We learned later in the day that the assassin was a Jewish Israeli. Still, the West Bank was immediately "sealed"—no one without an Israeli identity card was allowed inside Israel—for "security reasons." My family and neighbors in the village watched the funeral proceedings carefully; I wrote in my field notes that responses to Rabin's death were largely "cautious": certainly no one admitted sadness, but obvious happiness at his fate was also absent. The villagers with whom I spent my time wondered who and what would come next, and what this event would mean for them and their families.

Rabin's assassination, however, did not end the optimism for peace. From a different vantage point but one worth noting here, Ari Shavit, in an article in *The New Yorker*, described what the clientele looked like at this time from inside Jerusalem's famous King David Hotel:

> [In 1994 and 1995] you could actually see a new Middle East taking shape just by walking through the lobby. There were guests from the Gulf States in gold-embroidered gowns, and Hashemite guests in their red-white-and-black kaffiyehs, and C.E.O.s from almost every multinational corporation—Sony, Nokia, Mercedes.
>
> On November 4, 1995, dozens of heads of state attending the funeral of Prime Minster Yitzhak Rabin stayed at the hotel: King Hussein of Jordan, President Mubarak of Egypt, former United States Presidents Bush and Carter, and many of the European leaders. Prince Charles had to take a junior suite that night, because Bill and Hillary Clinton had already reserved the royal one. It was the last time a group like this would assemble in the hotel. (Shavit 2002: 59)

Indeed, the potential of this period for a peaceful future continued to seem great.

Shimon Peres continued the path to Palestinian autonomy outlined by Rabin and Arafat. The "smooth transition to Peres after Rabin's assassination, and Israeli public reaction to this event, increased Palestinian hope that Israel might be serious about reaching a genuine peace" (Rabbani 1996: 4). In December, a number of Palestinian cities were "liberated" from the Israelis, including Ramallah, Nablus, and Bethlehem. Everyone who could walk from Artas gathered in Bethlehem—old and young, men and women—to dance in the streets. A jubilant crowd tore down the barbed wire walls surrounding Deheisha and the walls of the Israeli police station in Bethlehem's main square. Flags were hung on the roofs of most houses in the village and everywhere in the streets. The celebrations were similar in Ramallah and Nablus.

Preparations for the first-ever Palestinian elections for an 88-member Palestinian Council and of Yassir Arafat as the *ra'is*, or chairman (or president), of the Palestinian Executive Authority soon followed, and many of the flags were replaced by a bewildering array of posters belonging to 33 candidates. The Bethlehem area was allotted four council seats. Voting stations were established in most villages; Artas had two, one in the boys' school and one in the kindergarten (no Artasis ran as candidates). I estimated that approximately half the village voted, with a ratio of 2:1 for male to female voters. Of the six villagers appointed to be observers, there was one woman.

The mood in Palestine after these elections was described as "poste-uphoric" by Mustafa Barghouti who wrote:

> People were eager to participate in the process and against all their experience and better judgment wanted to believe that we had entered a new stage, that elections would result in a structure of inclusion, and that the council would become a platform for the democratic expression of diverse views. They wanted to believe that the elections would open the way for an improved economic situation and a return to normal life. (1996: 87)

New members of the Palestinian police quickly replaced Israeli soldiers in the area, although the Israelis remained in control of the checkpoint into Jerusalem. It was an exciting time in the West Bank, a time when peace felt reachable. Palestinian flags which had not been permitted under Israeli occupation were proudly displayed from houses, and I believe there was an increased sense of national pride.

In March 1996, Hamas claimed responsibility for four suicide attacks that killed a total of fifty Israelis in late February and early March. The closure on the West Bank was tight and lasted for weeks. Some Artasis' reactions to the bombings included satisfaction: villagers would explain to me that they themselves had suffered even more terrible losses than those suffered by the Israelis because of the bus bombs. Other villagers declared that it was a shame (lit. *ḥarām*) to attack those not directly responsible (i.e., soldiers and government officials). While we saw no Israeli soldiers in the village, the closure was of a "new and unprecedented kind," cutting off West Bank communities from one another as well as the rest of the world with devastating economic consequences (Barghouti 1996: 88).

One commentator noted that the "high point of the DOP" lasted from the signing of Oslo II to the time of these suicide bombings (Rabbani 1996: 4), a period of time encompassed by my fieldwork. Not long after the bombings, in May 1996, conservative Benjamin Netanyahu was elected to be Israel's new Prime Minister. The Jewish settlement population in the West Bank continued to grow throughout 1996, contributing to villagers' fears that peace would remain elusive. The aura of hope and optimism that had framed the initial months of my fieldwork was diminished, although not gone. The election of the conservative Israeli government coincided with many villagers' realization of the difficulties facing the newly elected Palestinian officials. The Palestinian elected leadership struggled to make progress in building a Palestinian civil society, but found itself handcuffed by a lack of resources, vague definitions of the relationships among and responsibilities of the various political arms (including the Palestinian Authority Executive Authority, the PLO Executive Committee, the elected Palestinian Council, and the Palestinian National Council), Arafat's autocratic style of governing, and, of course, Israeli intransigence.

One analyst argued that calling this process a "peace process" was a mis-
nomer. He suggested a better term—Decolonization:

> A process whereby a new political entity is created out of the territorial con-
> traction of a presently existing one, [which] has historically been a difficult,
> brutal and bloody process. . . . The outcome of decolonization has usually
> been neo-colonialism—that is, continued domination by the former rulers
> through mostly economic rather than mostly political means. (Peled 1995:
> 14)

Another commentator argued that this "peace process" resulted in the creation of a series of "'arabistans,' ruled by a native authority, but subject to
overall Israeli control" (Rabbani 1996: 6). While Israeli soldiers were less
visible and Palestinian flags flew freely in Artas, the experience of domination and oppression continued, if somewhat less immediately than in the recent past.

I left Artas in early September 1996. Although the larger political events
I have described here were key to my fieldwork and its development, for
most women in the village, daily life continued largely uninterrupted in
any dramatic sense, although, of course, women experienced concern and
anxiety when contemplating their still uncertain political and economic fu-
tures. The changing political context often left men unemployed and at
loose ends in the village. In this respect, the men's daily rhythms were
more greatly disrupted than those of women. Cash flow quickly became a
problem for families during periods of closure, and men often felt that they
had failed in their responsibility to provide for their families. While villagers struggled with these feelings and experiences, they also pointed out,
with some relief, that they no longer saw Israeli soldiers in the village or
in Bethlehem, and that they had a police force of which they could be
proud.

Even after I left Artas in 1996 through the late 1990s, peace looked
somewhat possible depending, of course, on your perspective. Hope that the
process begun by Oslo would lead to true Palestinian autonomy was kept
alive for many Palestinians by the Palestinian leadership's claims "that the
concessions of the interim period would be recompense by iron resolve during the final status talks" (Hammami and Hilal 2001: 5). But in September
2000, the spark for the fire of the second intifada was nonetheless ignited,
easily aided by Ariel Sharon's now infamous visit to the Temple Mount, reflecting the growing anger and frustration of Palestinians in face of the fact
of ongoing Israeli occupation. The window of opportunity to be an American researcher of Jewish background living in a Muslim village in the Palestinian West Bank had mostly closed.

* * *

The relationships among stories of the jinn, social geography, and Israeli domination are drawn out most centrally in two of the following chapters: in my discussions of a jinn story in the context of the relationships of villagers to faraway family members in the Palestinian diaspora (chapter 4) and to those neighbors who are now uncomfortably close, the Jews (chapter 5). Yet Israeli domination of Palestinian life is not always at the foreground of this work. Chapter 3 looks at the experiences of some women who remain un-married, their experiences with the jinn, and how they are lost in the social geography of village life; their stories reflect on the complexity of familial re-lations and the social mores that require women to marry to become adults. An examination of the moral practices married women must publicly—in view of their neighbors and the jinn—demonstrate, including literal and sym-bolic cleanliness and fertility are also included here. Those who find it diffi-cult or impossible to fulfill these moral practices often know their difficulties to be caused by a jinn. Most immediately, commonly known knowledge about the jinn and their world, including appropriate treatment for those af-flicted by the jinn, is the subject of the following chapter, setting the stage for the chapters to follow.

NOTES

1. Transliterations used follow the guidelines of the *International Journal of Middle Eastern Studies* and/or are commonly used spellings in the literature on Palestinians.

2. See Seger (1981) for a published collection of Granqvist's photos from Artas.

3. See Moors (1995: 190-213) for a discussion of gender and garment production in the West Bank.

4. All villagers' names used are pseudonyms, with the exceptions of well-known individuals, such as Musa Sanad, who wished for their real names to be used. Place names are unchanged. Identifying individuals at the present time in Artas based on a reading of this text is impossible, as every family discussed in the following chapters has changed considerably since the time of my fieldwork (in terms of its composition, employment, etc.).

5. For a discussion of the history of the *kufiya* as well as its significance see Swedenburg (1990).

6. Ted Swedenburg, reflecting on his fieldwork in the West Bank on Palestinians' memories of the 1936–1939 Palestinian revolt against the British, argues his inter-views were "punctuated by significant silences and resistances, the passing over of is-sues that might project the 'wrong' image of the 1936–1939 revolt and expose the faultlines of the society" (1989: 268). The dominant discourses feared by these Pales-tinians interviewees were those of Israeli and American politicians and academics

who stress Palestinian factionalism and political backwardness to deny Palestinian national history and future statehood. Here I refer to dominant discourses propagated by those both within and outside of the village setting; it is the stories of the jinn which fill the "silences" and thus "expose the faultlines."

7. See el-Messiri (1978) for a discussion of *banat al-balad*, "daughters of the country," and references to her work on ibn al-balad in Cairo.

8. H. Geertz also notes that the terms *qarīb, qaraba*, and *quraba* are used in Morocco; according to one informant, the various forms of the word mean the "near ones." Geertz explained, "For him, as for some other speakers, the term *quraba* meant 'all close relatives,' including maternal kin and, probably, some affines or even non-relatives who have long been household members" (1979: 359).

9. Other kinds of historical circumstances result in similar outcomes for patterns of friendship. Wikan, for example, argues that in the case of Sohar, where women's lives are strictly defined by patterns of sex segregation and remaining far from the public eye, women maintain circles of diverse friends with their neighbors. Wikan argues, "the very diversity [in terms of ethnicity, age and wealth] of these circles indicates that physical closeness and convenience are major considerations in their formation" (1982: 116). Altorki similarly notes for elite women in Saudi Arabia, "compatibility of character and closeness of residence influence one's choice of preferred partners" (1986: 102). Joseph (1978: 545) argues that for women in an urban lower-class neighborhood in Lebanon the requirements of men's work away from their neighborhood left the street a female domain; for women, "co-residence in a street became a basis for intimacy." In these situations, as in Artas, the factor of physical proximity is made central in forming friendships.

10. See Rothenberg 1999b for a discussion of the relationships among Palestinian villages and those in the diasporas of Kuwait, Amman, and Toronto.

11. See Widen (1998) for a discussion of Granqvist's academic career following her research in Artas.

12. This is the transliteration of the magazine's name used by the magazine itself.

13. I did not gather statistics for literacy for villagers in Artas. Heiberg (1994:135), noting that "most international definitions of functional literacy take the ability to write, rather than to read, as the pivotal threshold [for determining literacy]," reports that 57 percent of females in the West Bank can write, 11 percent can write with difficulty, and 32 percent cannot write; for men in the West Bank, 77 percent can write, 15 percent can write with difficulty, and 8 percent cannot write.

14. The Applied Research Institute-Jerusalem states that the Artas population is 2679 ("Report about violated and confiscated lands in Artās [*sic*] village." 10 February 2003).

15. At the time of my fieldwork, villagers who obtained the necessary permission forms could cross the Israeli checkpoint to go to Jerusalem; permissions were often given to married men who had work inside Israel and women who demonstrated that they have a pressing reason (e.g., a hospital visit). Jerusalem identity cards are carried by Palestinians born inside Israel's pre-1967 borders and allow these Palestinians to cross freely to and from occupied territory and Israel.

16. The United Nations Relief and Works Agency (UNRWA) for Palestine Refugees in the Near East reports that the number of registered refugees in Deheisha in June 1996 was 8,237; however, UNRWA further claims that, "The figures on registered Palestinian refugees are not to be regarded as comprehensive demographic data . . . there are Palestine refugees in the area who are not registered with UNRWA although they have that entitlement" (Map of UNRWA's area of operations, June 30, 1996).

Chapter Two

The Jinn

King Solomon had power over the jinn; he was, in fact, their king as well as the king of the human world. So when King Solomon decided to build Solomon's Pools just a short walk from Artas, he ordered the jinn to do the necessary labor. Obedient to their king, the jinn worked and worked, digging the pools and lining them with stone. In the meantime, King Solomon sat and watched, leaning on his staff.

Unbeknownst to the jinn, King Solomon actually died one day as he sat on his chair leaning on his staff. Only forty years later, when the progress of worms eating his staff finally left the king to tumble to the ground, was the truth known. Set free of their labor, which was practically complete anyway, the jinn fled to Artas. So, you see, of the 100 jinn that live in the world, 99 of them live in Artas.

—Mr. Sanad, historian of Artas

The historical precedent for jinn stories in Artas is examined in this chapter, allowing us to reflect on transgenerational concerns and issues pertaining to the jinn and morality for villagers. Fortune-telling that relies upon the jinn for its success is worth exploring as well, as young people often are involved in this practice. This chapter then turns to a discussion of the current state of indigenous theory, methods, and treatment for the jinn, providing a necessary framework for understanding the jinn stories in the chapters that follow.

GRANQVIST AND THE JINN

Stories of the jinn are part of the historical tradition in Artas. The remarkable and detailed works of Finnish anthropologist Hilma Granqvist on village life in Artas (1931, 1935, 1947, 1950, and 1965) included a small number of jinn stories.

Several of the stories I collected resonate with the material Granqvist recorded in terms of their moralizing tone. While I do not want to over-interpret Granqvist's material—she provides little detailed context for the role of possession in the life of the possessed or for how the stories were told, and few details as to the shape, form, or character of the jinn themselves—her stories provide an important, if sketchy, historical backdrop for possession stories in Artas today. Perhaps Granqvist did not find certain details about the jinn and possession to be important, or, more likely, the jinn stories at the time did not include the well-defined individual characters or the kinds of dramatic possession episodes that are often shared in the village today.

Granqvist's limited stories of the jinn, as well as jinn stories originally recorded by Louise Baldensperger and Grace Crowfoot[1] in Artas the early 1930s (see Barghouti 1987) share some characteristics. Granqvist's materials suggest that the possessed were primarily women who exhibited impious and/or immodest behavior. The jinn were also believed to be a source of sickness who were drawn especially to vulnerable young children. The origins of the jinn were explained to Granqvist by Alya, one of her key informants, in this way:

According to a tradition the demons are a kind of degraded men. Eve is said to have felt so ashamed of her unbelievable fertility that she would not admit to having more than half the number of her children and tried to hide the rest. This only created enmity between the two groups and their descendants for all time.

Alya: Eve had forty in her womb.

Our father Adam asked her: "Where are thy children?" She said: "Those are my children."—Twenty were to be seen and twenty were hidden.

He said to her: "What is seen shall remain visible and what is hidden shall remain hidden." The latter became demons, Jinn, living invisible under the earth.

The demons are thus descendants of the children whom Eve was ashamed of acknowledging to Adam, because she had so many. (1950: 101)[2]

To explain patterns of possession among the villagers, Granqvist wrote:

Women are more in danger of being attacked by demons than are men. For instance, in connection with sexual intercourse, especially if it takes place out-of-doors; for instance in the garden, when not protected by their clothing, when bathing, when easing nature, and in many other instances in daily life. The demons are present everywhere and always ready to seize the opportunity of harming someone. People are able to protect themselves by repeating a formula of protection, the name of God, a prayer, or begging pardon. And man must be careful not to injure the demons. The name of God, or begging pardon is a warning to the demons to withdraw in time, so as not to be injured. (1965: 32)

The jinn were believed to be close guardians of propriety. Granqvist wrote:

They [the jinn] do not keep to their province under the earth. They envy the human beings who can live on the earth, and try to hurt and irritate them. For this reason people must be on their guard not to offend them. Otherwise they will take their revenge. People must always remember that they have the demons beneath them. (1950: 101)

Failure to maintain both propriety and piety—here often equated (cf. Meneley 1996)—is the cause of certain episodes of possession by the jinn. Specifically, forgetting to recite the proper blessings before certain acts, such as baking bread (Granqvist 1950: 100), bathing, or having sexual intercourse (1950: 101), or performing such acts in an improper place or manner may provide opportunities for the jinn to attack. For example, Granqvist describes a case of a woman who had sexual relations with her husband under a fig tree without asking Allah's forgiveness (for being in a public place) or blessing (as is necessary before having intercourse). The wife was afterwards subject to "fits." The woman and a sheikh who specialized in driving the jinn out of humans went into seclusion with certain foods necessary for obtaining the presence of the jinn. After demanding to speak with the jinn possessing the woman, Granqvist was told that the sheikh and the jinn had the following conversation:

The sheikh said: "What dost thou want from this woman?" The demon said: "I did not come to her, she came to me." The sheikh said: "How was that?" He answered: "I was sitting beneath the fig-tree and beneath me was the water. She came, she and her husband. Did they have to step on me? Her husband got up, and I went in to her." He said to the demon: "Get out of her!" The demon replied "I shall not come out." (1965: 29-30)

After some struggle between the sheikh and the jinn, including afflicting the sheikh with many plagues, the sheikh gave up and another was consulted. Eventually, the woman died. Granqvist first mentioned this story in 1947: 31.

In the Islamic world, "pious utterances frame all mundane activities, encapsulating them in sacred order and investing them with morality" (Lambek 1990: 23). Failing to recite the prescribed utterances, therefore, may threaten not only the morality of the individual, but also the social order in which that individual is enmeshed. Thus Granqvist described the jinn's ability to take offence over spilled water without uttering the name of Allah:

Sheikha, the wife of Musa Ahmad, was possessed by a spirit. She went to wash herself in a corner; she sprinkled hot water over herself; it fell on the face of the demon; she neither asked his pardon nor begged to be excused. From the day the hot water had been spilt on the floor, she had had epileptic fits. They brought the sheikh to her. He said to her people: "The woman went inside, washed herself in a corner, and sprinkled hot water which fell on the face of the demon." The demon said: "She sprinkled me with boiling water and I struck her in a rage." The sheikh said to the demon: "Come out of her!"—"I will not come out of her! Either she dies or I die." The demon died. (1965: 31-2)

A jinn may not always be evil. In a story gathered by Crowfoot and Baldensperger, the daughter of the Sultan of the jinn prevents a man from killing himself, and in the process teaches him a valuable lesson summarized in the proverb "A day in the world rather than a thousand under" (Barghouti 1987: 192–93). In this story, the jinn was summoned to the man by Allah; Allah wanted the man to understand that only God himself determines when a man should die. The jinn teaches the human this lesson.

During my fieldwork I was told a story by a young woman that I later learned was a near-verbatim recounting of a tale recorded by Crowfoot and Baldensperger (published by Barghouti). In this story a pious married woman is tested by holy men who have the power to see what the jinn are doing below the ground. These men arrive unannounced at the couple's home, and the wife immediately runs to make bread for the guests. Even in her haste, however, she does not forget at any point in her preparations to say the name of Allah. The holy men laughed at the site of the hungry jinn "waiting to snatch away some of the good things, but never a bite of food could they get" (Barghouti 1987: 145). When the woman's husband saw the men laughing, however, he assumed it was due to some fault of his wife. When the holy men left, the man divorced his wife.

After the man had remarried, the holy men came again. The men found the house messy and the wife reluctant to stop her work to offer her guests food. The holy men "saw the hungry spirits waiting, and as the wife took out the flour and *samn* [oil], and the rest, of each good thing they [the spirits] seized a part, and stuffed themselves and filled their leather bags until they were like to burst and at last, saving your presence, they broke wind with the weight of all they ate" (Barghouti 1987: 145-46). When the holy men asked the husband the whereabouts of his first wife and learned that he had divorced her, the holy men explained that they had been laughing at the pitiable state of the spirits. He then divorced his second wife and brought back his first.

This story is notable for two reasons. First, it demonstrates remarkable historical continuity (across more than seventy years) and emphasizes the point that while certain types of jinn stories reflect new characteristics, other threads of jinn stories are part of a long historical tradition in Artas. Indeed, first recorded in the 1920s and told to me in the 1990s, the story demonstrates remarkable longevity. While I cannot know if the story holds the same meaning for villagers who hear it now as it did for the villagers who heard it in Granqvist's time, it is nonetheless suggestive of the importance of this particular moral point across time. Second, this tale further demonstrates that while women may be the primary targets of the jinn, a pious woman may prevent their attack and win the admiration of holy men. Few stories that I collected about the jinn emphasized a woman's superior moral worth and her husband's foolishness, yet this is one story that has endured.

I gathered many stories that are similar in their moralistic tone to others recorded nearly seventy years ago. In Artas today, immodest or impious behavior is still understood to be a pathway for an attack by the jinn. For example, being harsh with children may make the children vulnerable to possession by the jinn. One woman told me she once slapped her small son on his cheek. His mouth froze in place and did not move until he was treated by a sheikh. The sheikh told her that the jinn had entered the little boy's mouth at the precise place where she had hit him. Children in Artas are not expected to be reasonable or, therefore, punishable for their misdeeds. Reasonableness and the capacity for exercising discipline occur when a child is able to grasp the intricacies of social relations and put that knowledge into practice. Punishing a child too severely is believed to be unseemly for reasonable (i.e., socialized) adults, and partially socialized beings such as children should be treated with kindness and indulgence. According to the sheikh, therefore, the jinn attacked the little boy as a warning to his mother to treat her son with greater understanding, an attribute that is considered part of a pious and moral woman's behavior.

In a similar vein but turning our attention to the propriety of men, a story that now circulates in Artas concerns a man who had to urinate during a wedding celebration. Too lazy to walk to his home, he simply urinated on the outside wall of the building in which the party was being held. Afterwards, he immediately felt a pain in his head and chest. His family took him to many doctors, but none was able to help. His family eventually took him to a sheikh who determined that his choice to urinate in public was indeed the reason for his affliction and who was able to force the female jinn, or jinnia, to leave him. In another tale, a man in his sixties told me that he and two friends visited some prostitutes in Jerusalem many years ago. After falling asleep with the prostitute the man was awakened by something invisible hitting him on the face. The beating only stopped once he had left the brothel. He immediately consulted a sheikh who told him that the jinn who beat him was a jinnia who would no longer bother him if he promised to stop seeing prostitutes.

Other kinds of undesirable behavior may merit punishment from the jinn, such as exhibiting greed or carelessness. A neighbor of mine in Artas worked with a man who was hit by a jinn after he looked down a well for some valuables which he had heard were hidden there. This man argued that a jinn hit him in the back of the neck because he was specifically looking for the treasure.[3] A jinn may also take the form of an animal. A story I heard numerous times in Artas concerned a man who carelessly ran over a rabbit who was a jinn. The responsible man was then "worn," or possessed, by the jinn as punishment until a sheikh could finally persuade the jinn to leave. Similarly, I heard stories about both men and women who, after unceremoniously shooing away a cat who was in fact a jinn, were possessed and had to be treated by a sheikh.

Today, as in Granqvist's time, many villagers consult sheikhs about their ill-nesses (particularly in cases of infertility, discussed in chapter 4). Sickness, Granqvist noted, was believed to be a warning or punishment from Allah or his demons, or the result of witchcraft done by those who were envious or jeal-ous (1965: 23-4). A sheikh might drive out the jinn from a person who is pos-sessed, by using his own skills or mobilizing the help of a jinn who works for him (Granqvist 1965: 28–29). The relationship of sickness and possession is still a common theme in Artas. Villagers often told me that after seeing nu-merous doctors for an undiagnosable feeling of malaise, they were finally cured by the attentions of a sheikh.

These perennial tales about the jinn are moralistic and predictable and demonstrate the greatest continuity in form and content to those gathered by Granqvist, Crowfoot, and Baldensperger. We are provided with the episode that caused the possession, its resolution, and an explanation. The stories sug-gest an enduring, transgenerational concern with the maintenance of proper behavior that is governed by villagers' changing understandings of piety and morality. Villagers' commentaries on the risks of possession entailed in treat-ing children or animals with harshness, for example, round out some of the finer points of proper behavior and reason, and emphasize that morality is a public concern. Forgetting to recite the name of God when one has no human witnesses, or performing a private act in a public space were, and still are to-day, sinful acts that risk punishment from a watchful spirit world. In addition to the public and practical demonstrations of cleanliness and fertility required before one's neighbors, piety and propriety must be demonstrated before the jinn, even inside one's own home.

Jinn stories complicate simple notions of public and private space in village life. It has been recognized that public space in Middle Eastern societies is not necessarily space that belongs to men and is associated with power and institu-tionalized politics; nor is private space only the "women's world" and associ-ated solely with domestic concerns (Nelson 1974; cf. Rosaldo 1974). In light of the omnipresence of the jinn in village life, public and private spaces are places of greater or lesser exposure to others, marking opposing ends of a social spec-trum that never totally allows an individual—man or woman—to be alone. To-day, as at the time of Granqvist's research, private space may not be private at all, if it is believed to be shared with spirits who await the opportunity to pun-ish a human for his or her improper behavior. Yet, not realizing when an act should be carried out in a more private space, or at least a space less publicly visible to one's human neighbors, also merits punishment from the jinn.

Based on Granqvist's work and other historical materials, it is possible to theorize that many aspects of morality—especially concerns about proper comportment in terms of pious behavior before the watchful eyes of the jinn—are long-standing, historical aspects of moral behavior in Artas. This historical record from within Artas helps to provide a framework within which to situate and compare contemporary young women's lives and their experiences with the jinn. We thus learn, in specific instances, of aspects of morality that may have been maintained across the generations and that link cultural practices in Artas today to those of the recent past (cf. Yanagisako and Collier 1987: 46).

THE JINN TODAY

Differences between specific stories that I collected about the jinn and those recorded in the 1920s suggest ways in which village social life and the jinn discourse has changed over time. These changes reflect on villagers' perceptions of, responses to, and experiences with new social realities and a variety of hegemonic structures.

It is well known by villagers today that the jinn are eminently social creatures, living in a world that parallels our own, invisible to us, and able to see and enter our world freely. As social creatures, the jinn have changed, much as the village and its occupiers have changed in the past 100 years. The jinn are more self-conscious of their identities and the boundaries of those identities than they were a century ago. They often have religious beliefs. In their own world, the jinn are often involved in struggles with one another to achieve power and control, they have wars and armies, and they engage in negotiations and create treaties; in the human world, they are offended not only by human lapses in the traditional moral code, such as forgetting to recite a blessing, but also by human fallibility in maintaining proper moral behavior in the post-colonial, pseudo-post-occupation world. Such "modern" threats may include the temptation of Israeli women's reputed sexual freedom—a freedom as much a threat to Palestinian women as to Palestinian men, although for different reasons.

Jinn today may choose to fully possess a human, moving his or her limbs, or simply to "haunt" an individual, bringing bad luck and ill fortune. They may be gotten rid of by a sheikh, a Muslim holy man, who will engage in prolonged readings of the Qu'ran near the afflicted person. Ideally, the sheikh will persuade the jinn to speak through the person, identify its demands, and reach an agreement for the jinn's departure. Today villagers believe that the jinn can take a variety of shapes, from human to animal.[4] A jinn may appear to the one he wants to possess but does not inevitably do so. People may experience possession by or contact with the jinn in varying degrees of intensity. Humans may have friendships or love relationships with a jinn. Female jinnia are believed to be particularly forceful and persuasive in pursuing a love affair with a human man.

The world of the jinn is generally believed to be perfectly parallel to our own. The primary difference is that the jinn are able to move between their world and ours, while we cannot. A 13-year-old boy wrote the following for me when I asked his class to write what they knew about the jinn in a brief essay:

> The jinn as we know it is a type of creature created by Allah from flames of fire. They can enter the bodies of humans without differentiating among young or old, women or men, Muslims or unbelievers. There are many reasons they may enter a person's body. For example, if a jinnia loves a human and wants to marry him. Or the opposite may happen, the jinn may enter a person for revenge if the person spilt water without saying the name of Allah, or if a person bothers a jinn. Sometimes a jinn may be sent by one of the Samaritans to cause troubles for human beings. Sometimes a jinn may bother one who is envied. Protecting yourself from the jinn is far easier than the treatment for getting rid of the jinn.

Many villagers believe each jinn has a religion, most commonly Judaism, Christianity, Islam, and idol-worship (or fire worship).[5] The Jewish and idolatrous jinn are generally believed to be the worst kind of jinn, while the religious Muslim jinn are the least troublesome for human beings. As Kahana notes about *zar* (a type of jinn) in Ethiopia, "the parallelism between the *Zar* spirit world and the human world enables the former to be comprehended by the latter" (1985: 129).

The maintenance of proper village morality is central in many jinn stories today, as it was in Granqvist's time. Indeed, jinn are often implicated in women's failure to adhere to the moral requirements of morality and fertility. Yet jinn stories today also provide a subtle means of articulating and reflecting on the multifaceted nature of the relationships among occupier and occupied, and families in the West Bank and those in diaspora. These issues are explored in later chapters.

TREATMENT

According to villagers, diagnosing a jinn can be a tricky matter, and jinn possession is often misdiagnosed by trained medical doctors. Difficulty in diagnosing the jinn is in part due to the obstacles in determining why a jinn has afflicted a particular person. At times, possession may be clearly related to an offense against the jinn; in other instances, a person may be a victim of magic. Few people claim to know exactly how magic that brings the jinn is done, but many who have had troubles with the jinn argue that they were the victims of this kind of magic. Magic here is a vague term referring to a threatening force, the presumed capacity of one's neighbors or acquaintances, but never one's self.[6]

The possessed are generally young men and women; one sheikh who treats the jinn hypothesized:

> The jinn wear all people, but the majority are women. It is about 60 or 70 percent women, 10 to 15 percent children, and the rest are men. There are more women who are worn by the jinn because they are jealous from each other. If a woman is married to a man that another woman loves, that other women will make magic for the first one, and so on. In most cases the jinn comes by magic, rarely for revenge.

The stories I collected about the jinn suggest that the majority of the possessed are women, but men's stories of possession can also often be heard (these are explored in chapter 5). Here I discuss two different approaches taken by specialists to rid the afflicted of the jinn.

Ahmad

In the Bethlehem area there is a young man, whom I will call Ahmad, who is particularly well-known for his ability to treat the jinn. He is often consulted by the people of Artas and regularly comes to the village or invites them to his home for treatment sessions. In his final year at Bethlehem University he wrote an extensive tract on the proper diagnosis and treatment of the jinn for his "senior essay." Ahmad majored in psychology; his essay on the jinn, written for a religious Christian professor, did not receive a good grade. Yet Ahmad has distributed copies of his paper widely among his fellow students and hopes someday to publish it as part of the literary jinn genre, so it may be used as a manual for sheikhs engaged in the treatment of those possessed by the jinn. During numerous interviews we read through Ahmad's draft together. I have permission to cite it, using his pseudonym, here. I combine this information from Ahmad with my own observations of treatment sessions.

When a person is suspected or known by his/her family members to be possessed by a jinn, he or she will come to Ahmad. Ahmad's first step is to ask the allegedly possessed person the following questions about his sleeping behavior:

Do you spend the night in sleeplessness?
Do you see visions in the night?
Do you have terrible dreams?
Do you see animals in the bedroom?
Do you grind your teeth in your sleep?
Do you laugh or cry while sleeping?
Do you cry out in your sleep?
Do you stand and walk while sleeping?
Do you feel as though you fell from a high place while lying on your bed?

Do you see yourself in a tomb or garbage can?
Do you see people in strange shapes?
Do you see ghosts?

In addition, Ahmad advises the sheikh to ask questions about the patient's behavior while awake:

Do you always have a headache and cannot find any medical treatment for it?
Do you forget to mention the name of Allah?
Are you continuously distracted?
Are you weak and lazy?
Are you epileptic, with convulsions or attacks of the nerves?

Not all of the questions have to be answered affirmatively; a few affirmative answers are enough for a diagnosis of possession. While some kind of physical ailment is usually necessary for the patient to be widely acknowledged as possessed (although not all physical ailments are understood as evidence of possession), this ailment must be coupled with the certainty of the patient or her family that she is possessed. This certainty is more important than any other single physical factor.

There are three stages of treatment once a diagnosis of possession has been established. First, the room in which the treatment will take place must be properly prepared. At no stage during treatment is music, drumming, or dance involved, as they are in other parts of the Middle East and North Africa;[7] such practices are, in fact, explicitly forbidden. All pictures must be removed from the walls and hidden, as should all musical instruments or tapes. The sick person's existing amulets should be removed and burned. All evidence of impiety, such as a man wearing gold jewelry or a woman wearing makeup or not wearing a head covering, must be corrected.

For the next phase of treatment, the sheikh reads verses from the Qu'ran close to the ear of the patient.[8] Many sheikhs whom I observed read into a microphone attached to a stereo system. Earphones are given to the patient, and the volume of the sheikh's voice is turned up as high as possible. This is supposed to provide the utmost effect. If no stereo system is available, however, simply reading the Qu'ran near the sick person in a loud and clear voice is sufficient. After an unspecified period of reading Qu'ran (which may last twenty minutes or hours), the sheikh will then ask the jinn to leave the body of the afflicted. If all goes well, the jinn will immediately agree (this may be indicated by the jinn speaking through the human body it has possessed or the person him/herself relaying the message from the jinn that the spirit has agreed to leave). This can be a very problematic part of the procedure, however, and often the sheikh must enter into long and protracted arguments with the jinn before persuading the spirit to leave the body. It is at this point that the sheikh may learn about the particular identity of the jinn and force his/her conversion to Islam.

The sheikh may learn that more than one jinn is afflicting the individual; I heard stories of hundreds of jinn possessing a person simultaneously. In the midst of one treatment session I observed, the sheikh paused and explained the following to me:

> This boy that I am treating here has 21 jinn. Eight want to become Muslims and we want to kill 13. I gave the eight the chance to become Muslims and let them leave the body. If they become Muslim I let them leave and then I will kill the others.

The sheikh may, in addition to conversion, attempt to kill the offending spirit with jinn who work on his behalf (as a kind of personal army), or, most simply, expel the jinn. If the jinn are expelled, they are known to leave through the fingertips or toes of the afflicted. Once the jinn have been successfully expelled, the sheikh may then spray the face of the afflicted with water he has blessed prior to the treatment session and pronounce the patient to be cured.

The final phase of treatment is considered by Ahmad to be the most important. The previously possessed person must maintain a rigorously pious lifestyle. In particular, the person must remember to pray regularly, not to listen to music or television (particularly foreign songs or shows), read a verse from the Qu'ran daily, stay far away from those who are not religious, and, if the formerly possessed is a woman, to cover her head. If the person should return to his/her "old ways," ways that stray from ideas of what constitutes a pious, traditional Muslim lifestyle (according to Ahmad), and tend toward the adoption of foreign ideas, he/she risks being repossessed.

Treatment sessions such as Ahmad's and others that I witnessed usually lack a dramatic performance quality. They are private and relatively rare affairs, with only a few ritual or symbolic objects and witnesses. Treatment aims to rid the human body of the spirit, in contrast with spirit possession in other parts of the world where the treatment pacifies the spirit but the relationship with its human host is lifelong.[9] The spirit may or may not speak or act in any way through the body of the possessed; indeed, the possessed person may simply report feeling better after the treatment, a feeling that, if confirmed by family members, puts the matter to rest.

Ahmad added the following philosophical note during one of our interviews concerning his role as a sheikh who treats those afflicted by the jinn:

> The Qu'ranic treater must not take a position of authority over the sick person. The sick person must not feel that he is submitting or obeying a higher authority than his own wish. So the treater must explain his role to the sick person, so that if the treater asks the sick person for anything, the sick person will know that this request is for no other reason than his own health and happiness. So the Qu'ranic treater must place himself in the position of the sick person. He should

learn the sick person's personal circumstances, his pressures, and the crises with
which he may be living, so he may understand the reasons for the cruel and evil
attack from the jinn.

Here Ahmad is arguing for an equitable relationship between himself and the
afflicted; he is further recognizing that the "personal circumstances" of the
possessed have a great deal to do with her possession. This is not to state that
the jinn are not real for Ahmad: they are very real indeed and must be treated
with respect. Yet a jinn will rarely select a person to possess unless the person gives the jinn reason and opportunity. Ahmad aims to identify the locus
of the opportunity for the jinn and to help prevent further attacks.

Im Musa

Im Musa lives in a refugee camp outside of Nablus. I traveled to see this
sheikha with a middle-aged man from Artas whom I will call Muhammed
and with my research assistant. Muhammed was concerned that his daughter was "haunted" by the jinn, since no one had come to ask for her hand in
marriage. When the three of us traveled to Nablus, we asked people on the
street for the sheikha's location. We were quickly directed to her home, a
structure wedged between two cement-poured, newer-looking homes. When
we entered the house, we found ourselves in the living room of the sheikha,
a room lined with people sitting and standing waiting their turn to see her,
while the sheikha herself sat on a couch at one end of the room. Most of the
other people waiting, like the men from Artas with whom I came, held photos, and slightly more than half were women. The sheikha would take the
photo, place it under a prayer mat on the couch next to her, draw on small
pieces of paper, and place those also under the prayer mat while talking to
the people sitting in the room. A cordless telephone rang and she briefly consulted with a man who was phoning from America. She dealt with people
bluntly and curtly, yelling at one older woman that if she did not have a hun-
dred shekels, she could go home, as that was her final price for getting rid of
the magic done to the woman's daughter. After waiting for some time, she
would pull out from under the prayer mat a small stone which, she told the
room, the jinn had brought. She would then give the stone, the papers, and
the picture to the person whose turn it was at that moment, accompanied by
advice on what to do with each item.

Eventually, it was Muhammed's turn. The procedure was the same as for
the others. The jinn brought a triangular stone and the sheikha told
Muhammed to mix the stone with water and sugar and then wait. Soon, she
told him, someone would come to ask for his daughter's hand. Muhammed
paid her forty Jordanian dinars and then twenty more after she imperiously
shouted, "Sixty!!" We then left and returned to Artas.

Contrasting styles

For Ahmad and other curers like him, dealing directly and in detail with both the jinn and his patients' lifestyles is a key difference between his philosophy and the philosophy of other types of curers.[10] Im Musa may have messages brought to her by the jinn in the form of small stones, but she is neither interested nor involved in their conversions or their deaths. Nor is she overly concerned about how her patients live their lives at home, whether or not women cover their hair, and so on.

The differences between the two should not be seen as a simple result of gender or education. I saw men who practiced in very much the same way as Im Musa, and others who practice as Ahmad does without a formal university education, although they are trained to treat jinn cases through study and training with instructors such as Ahmad. Neither curers' patients can be characterized by age or urban or rural backgrounds. Perhaps in time each type of curer will come to appeal to increasingly specific and differentiated audiences, but at the time of my fieldwork that differentiation had not yet occurred. There is no question, however, that Ahmad's style is newer and quickly gaining ground. It remains to be seen if Im Musa and other practitioners similar to her will be able to maintain their practices.

The fact that Ahmad's style of curing for possession is rapidly spreading suggests the growing influence of Islamist forces in the West Bank. Of course, conservative Islamist trends have been observed in the Gaza Strip for some time. For example, young men have at times brutally enforced the wearing of headscarves by young women (see Hammami 1990). Yet this conservatism at the time of my fieldwork was typically not as explicitly visible to the same degree in the West Bank as it was in Gaza. It seems clear that the growth in popularity of Ahmad's approach to and understanding of the jinn was a clear foreshadowing of an increasingly conservative political and religious climate in the West Bank.

It is also interesting to note that, while Im Musa's style of curing may not be a consistently gendered one, it is possible that Ahmad's is. I did not meet any women who practiced as he does. Conservative Islamists in Gaza and in many other places in the Middle East have little room for publicly visible roles for women as religious leaders or healers. Seen by these conservative forces as improperly practicing Islam, women such as Im Musa are seriously frowned upon (at best). As the popularity of conservative Islamic leaders grows, it is very possible that Im Musa will find herself unable to practice; and the foreclosing of one kind of professional option for women—an option that is relatively financially successful in the West Bank—should not be taken lightly.

While specialists such as Ahmad and Im Musa have treated many possessed people, and I witnessed curing episodes, it is more common among Palestinians in the West Bank to hear about and discuss spirit possession events after the incident of possession rather than to witness them in process. I was told, however, that possession episodes involving a trance-like state in the West Bank are spontaneous. An individual who has experienced a trance state may not do so in the course of treatment. Often, those actively possessed by the jinn in Artas are believed to be possessed because they seem inexplicably distracted, sleepless, depressed, or surly. In these cases, the possessed is unaware of the jinn until it is pointed out by others.[11] These ongoing episodes of possession are in essence also primarily narrative events for villagers. Those who receive treatment for possession but do not believe themselves to be possessed may be more or less willing to receive treatment; often, if an individual is unwilling, he or she is pressured into treatment by concerned family and friends. Those who know and admit that they are possessed may demonstrate symptoms similar to those who do not believe themselves to be possessed, or exhibit (although relatively rarely) symptoms of spontaneous, trance-like behavior.

It is important to realize that cases of spirit possession are widely discussed by people in Artas, although they may occur relatively rarely. The greater social relevance of possession episodes, then, is in the telling and retelling of the events—the symbolic implications of "wearing" a jinn—not in the experiences themselves.

POSSESSED OR
MENTALLY ILL?

When no physical diagnosis can be made for a physical ailment, such as a stomach ache or back pain, possession by the jinn will often be blamed. Often, even when a doctor diagnoses a certain physical ailment (e.g., appendicitis or a pulled muscle), a sheikh may also be consulted in order to complement the doctor's orders.

A man who treats numerous jinn cases in the Bethlehem area told me the following:

> The jinn is a kind of epilepsy, a kind of imbalance. But there are two kinds of epilepsy. The first is a physical type which is related to the composition of the brain. In this type the brain is undeveloped although the body is developed and this affects the human. We can't treat this using the Qu'ran, but we can treat him by putting him in a special hospital. The second kind is the evil jinn which causes a human to be insane. We can treat this easily by using the Qu'ran. Some of these cases involve paralysis or infertility and these are caused by the jinn. But we can't say that all of these problems are always caused by the jinn. We must take these cases to physicians. If the doctor finds something wrong he is going to give medicine for the patient's treatment. But there is nothing wrong with also turning to the Qu'ran to help get rid of any jinn that may be there.

Physical ailments, therefore, may involve both medically diagnosable problems and the presence of the jinn. When confronted with a serious medical problem, I know of no villagers who would refuse to see a doctor and only consult a sheikh. If a doctor cannot locate and/or treat the problem in any way then consideration of the jinn slowly becomes the exclusive focus for the illness. In the majority of cases of physical complaints, however, a doctor's orders will be followed, accompanied by the ministerings of a sheikh.

In contrast to the complementary, relatively nonconflicting approaches of sheikh and doctor to physical ailments, the distinction between affliction by the jinn and mental illness in the Western sense is a topic of increasing debate in the West Bank and Gaza Strip. For example, in an extended article in the weekend supplement of *The Jerusalem Post*, a view of the relationship between society, politics, mental health, and possession by the jinn in Gaza was articulated by Palestinian psychiatrist Eyad Sarraj. Dr. Sarraj identified Gaza's political turbulence, including "the violent intifada and its suppression, the disorienting transition from the intifada to peace, and the transfer of power to the Palestinian Authority whose rule has already been marred by grave infringements of human rights" as some of the reasons behind many Gazans' mental health problems (paraphrased by Hecht 1996: 9). Yet Dr. Sarraj argues:

> "In Israel there is a tendency to separate politics from mental health. This separation is very artificial, because politics is part of the mental health of the individual and of the public. [Israelis] use a kind of objectivity from the Freudian school, as if the therapist must be and can be objective. But this is impossible, because no one is objective." (quoted by Hecht 1996: 13)

Dr. Sarraj clearly feels that the oppressive conditions of life in Gaza and the mental health of Gazans are deeply entwined, a relationship the Israelis often overlook. Dr. Sarraj's recognition of the importance of contextualizing the existence of mental problems in Gaza, however, does not include recognizing the role of sheikhs in "curing" patients of their problems.

Yet nearly all of the patients who come to Dr. Sarraj's Gaza Community Mental Health Program (GCMHP) have seen sheikhs first. In the report, Dr. Sarraj theorized that this is in large part due to social constraints:

> The stigma attached to mental illness in Gaza is just one of the powerful reasons those in need of help try other options first. Young women who undergo treatment risk never being able to marry. The disgrace may even destroy their sisters' chances of marriage.
>
> Men are unlikely to seek treatment because of a process of denial that helps them maintain their sense of strength or heroism. The extreme example is that of men violently abused while in detention in Israeli prison, who see themselves as heroes when they come out. "They are used to suppressing their feelings,

especially painful ones like grief," Sarraj says, and they have developed the "psychology of the victim," seeing whatever emotional problems they have as lying outside the self. (paraphrased and quoted by Hecht 1996: 9-10)

Dr. Sarraj further argues that Gazans are "generally ignorant of self and psychology" (quoted by Hecht 1996: 9), clearly referring to the concepts in the Western sense. Dr. Sarraj's most common cases among women include hysteria, hysterical dissociation, "the kind of personality split that is perceived as possession," and somatic complaints, including paralysis, blindness, and loss of voice (paraphrased by Hecht 1996: 11). Among men, Dr. Sarraj typically treats cases of delusions "often related to their honor, dignity or political loyalty."

Traditional healers can be useful, according to Dr. Sarraj, in cases "susceptible to suggestion," such as "wedding-night syndrome" (the sudden impotence of the groom) (quoted by Hecht 1996: 110). Yet, as Dr. Sarraj argues, more often than not, traditional healers exacerbate the patient's situation:

> Traditional healers see epileptics, for example, as people whose bodies have been inhabited by demons. Sarraj says he knows of epileptic women being raped, even beaten to death, by spiritual healers "trying to get the devil out." (paraphrased by Hecht 1996: 11)

Further, there are other kinds of cases of "possession" dealt with by sheikhs in ways Dr. Sarraj and his colleagues also consider unhelpful:

> But there are other kinds of "possession," according to Dr. Mustafa Masri, a psychiatrist who plans, supervises and evaluates clinical work at the GCMHP.
>
> A Moslem woman may wake up one day with an additional identity: as a Christian, a Jew or even an Israeli. This kind of splitting occurs in response to severe stress and is a way of coping with it, he says. But instead of receiving [psychiatric] treatment—especially if she is poorly educated and has a passive husband who can't protect her—she will be pushed into becoming a healer herself by a society that sees her as having acquired supernatural powers from the jinn—or demon—that has possessed her.
>
> The number of traditional healers, both male and female, is increasing, and even educated people line up for their services, says Masri [a Palestinian psychiatrist who also works at the GCMHP], who studied at the University of Alexandria. (Hecht 1996: 11)

Depending on local context, certain kinds of symptoms are "idiomatic of possession." These symptoms may include paralysis or blindness, among others (Boddy 1992: 328). In the Palestinian context, most of the symptoms described by Dr. Sarraj are considered by many villagers to be indicative of possession by the jinn and may be further considered "idioms of distress" (Nichter 1981) within the language of spirit possession. Possession "is a learned behavior whose manifestation is bound by implicit rules" (Boddy 1992: 324). People who demonstrate that they are competent within the prescribed rules of possession behavior are likely to be accepted as possessed. Mental retardation and insanity, for example, are not part of the jinn idiom in the West Bank, and in these cases sheikhs will not be consulted. These cases represent an indigenous category of incurable illnesses, believed to be determined by Allah in terms of both their cause and resulting effects. Villagers do not consider those so afflicted to be possessed by the jinn.

Some Palestinians have adopted Western-style, medicalized language and practice of mental health care. Yet as Taussig observes, this approach denies "the human relations embodied in symptoms, signs, and therapy, [thus] we not only mystify [these relations] but we also reproduce a political ideology in the guise of a science of (apparently) 'real things'—biological and physical thinghood" (1980: 3). Here Ahmad's emphasis on the afflicted one's "personal circumstances" in order to understand the reasons for attack by the jinn would be discarded and the symptoms themselves decontextualized.

It is perhaps because of the common difficulty in pinpointing the causes of mental disease that the relationship between sheikhs and mental health specialists is conflictual, particularly when compared to the relationship between sheikhs and doctors who treat the body. I recorded a debate between a woman, whom I will call Fatima here, who works as a nurse at one of the few mental health institutions in the West Bank, located in Bethlehem just down the road from Artas, and a man, called Muhammed here, whose sister endured one of Artas' most famous jinn cases. Here are excerpts of their discussion:

[Muhammed described a case of a boy who hit his head repetitively against a wall, but was finally cured of this behavior by a sheikh]

Fatima: Look, everything you are saying is useless—believe me. I have worked in the mental hospital for three years and we see a lot of cases every day. A lot of these people have gone to sheikhs before they came to the hospital. If you knew what a disaster it is—what the sheikhs do to these people you wouldn't believe. These people are sick, not wearing the jinn.

Muhammed: The sheikh who treated this boy studied for four years in the university [Muhammed is referring to Ahmad, above]. I mean, he was not somebody off the street. I mean, he won't even treat a woman who does not have her hair covered!

Fatima: We have some mentally ill people in the hospital and we ask them what they see, imagine, who is your enemy, who is your friend, what do you hear. Sometimes they say his wife or his sister is his enemy. Does this mean that he has a jinn? All of these things are sickness—not acts of the jinn.

Muhammed: I know a director of a mental health hospital who transferred a woman away from there to a sheikh, and the sheikh treated her. Even a doctor in Amman who tried to treat my sister told me to take her to a sheikh.

[here the conversation drifted]

A psychiatrist at this mental institution in Bethlehem emphasized to me that mental disorders are, in general, considered to be shameful for Palestinian families and that relatively few will consult a Western-trained medical specialist for such problems. Muhammed, however, is emphasizing his willingness to take his sister to see a doctor—and it was the doctor himself who admitted he could not help her. For villagers who do not accept the authority of mental health practitioners, Muhammed's experience confirms their implicit belief that mental health and publicly practiced morality are intimately bound together. A psychiatrist cannot begin to address these issues with prescriptions for drugs or individual therapy.

While there are villagers who claim not to believe in the jinn or the stories of those who claim to be possessed, most will admit to the possibility that possession can occur, if rarely. Interested as I am in the public assertions of the meaning of possession, I view the possession experience not as a symptom of mental illness, but as "an idiom for articulating a certain range of experience" (Crapanzano 1977a: 10). In contrast to Dr. Sarraj and a growing number of practicing psychiatrists in the West Bank, I think that spirit possession may best be understood along the lines of Crapanzano's assertion that it "provides an individual with an idiom for self-articulation which is oriented differently from the essentially internalized, past-suffused psychological idiom of the Western world" (1977a: 22). As discussed, the expression "to wear a jinn" indicates that possession by a jinn has external and public significance, just as a woman's clothing externalizes her social self, and her clean front porch externalizes the inside of her home to those who are familiar with village life.

FORTUNE-TELLING

Specialists in fortune-telling often operate with techniques similar to those of the sheikhs and may also be consulted for learning the human source of the magic that brought a troublesome jinn to an individual. One common method of fortune-telling is through the use of the *mandal*, a plate filled with water or oil.[12] A piece of cloth is then placed on the plate; the diviner stares at the cloth until he sees a jinn, who generally appears as a person. The jinn will then reveal the answers to the question being asked by the diviner. One elderly man in Artās told me how he had been used by a sheikh while he was a young man to speak with the jinn as they appeared in the *mandal*. The young man, it seemed, had a particular gift for being able to see and speak with the jinn. He told me about the following incident:

> I told the sheikh once about my sister's sickness. So the sheikh came and brought the plate and a white cloth and put oil on the plate and began to read

[the Qu'ran]. I could see the jinn in the plate – they are not different from us. My sister, they told me, was worn [possessed] by two jinn, one Muslim and one Christian. The Christian jinn went away when we read [the Qu'ran], but the Muslim insisted that he wanted to marry my sister. His eyelashes were more than ten centimeters long, he had hair like a gorilla, he was like a beast. We tried to get him to go away but he refused. When I saw him I was afraid of him, and I wanted to get out of the mandal, but the sheikh told me to stay. When the jinn refused to turn away from my sister the sheikh made him go to court, and they brought judges and hanged him [in the jinn world]. When I went home that night I saw that my sister was healthy again.

The tale is somewhat confusing: at first the jinn appear as humans, but later on one jinn appears as a frightening animal-like entity. Yet the story draws out many characteristics of jinn stories in and around Artas. First, the jinn involved have religious identities; second, the jinn world is in many ways similar to the human world (in this case the presence of courts, judges, and punishment is emphasized); and, third, the jinn is successfully expelled.

Another method of fortune-telling involves "reading" the grinds left in the bottom of a coffee cup, a *finjān*. The shapes of the grinds hold specific meanings; Saleh described some of the common meanings attributed to the particular shapes of the grinds:

> For example, a black shape means persons or places, white shapes mean roads or streets. For example, the reader may say, "You have a long road in front of you, or, you have a short road," if there was a black point cutting off the white point. Big points mean that some accident will happen to you. For example, the reader may say: "You are going to face a lot of problems, but you are going to overcome them, but you must be careful of your relatives. They are doing something to you, trying to stop your progress." (translation is mine, 1975: 98)

In addition to the reader's skills, a jinn may provide the *finjān* reader with additional interpretation, background, and insight by providing the reader with the necessary details (only the reader can "hear" the jinn's information).

Finjān reading is not as common in the Bethlehem area as it is in and around Ramallah. When I was in Ramallah I met a young woman at Bir Zeit University who told me the following story:

> I and five of my friends went to have our coffee cups read. We were four Muslims and one Christian. On the way there one of the Muslim girls and the Christian girl exchanged necklaces, one which had on it the word of God, Allah, and the other had a cross. When the woman read the first of the coffee cups she said things we couldn't believe—she would say a name, how the person with this name was related to her, and what the person with that name did. Then she started to read the grinds of the woman wearing the cross when we saw something trying to choke the reader. We were very frightened. Then the reader asked

the Muslim girl, "What's your religion? Because the jinn are trying to choke me!" The girl said, "I am a Muslim." Then the reader asked her to take off the cross so she could read the finjān; the reader couldn't read it for her if she was wearing the cross, the jinn wouldn't let her.

Here the jinn appear in order to maintain propriety, this time forbidding the blurring of religious identity boundaries. It is important here to realize that the girls were "wearing" inappropriate religious symbols. One *wears* markers of social identity, indicating the status of a social self. By switching their necklaces, a cross and the name of Allah, the girls were transgressing this social code of behavior and its significance. While each girl may each have been sure of her identity after the exchange of necklaces—believing they could maintain a sense of self separate from what they wore—this separation of external appearance and identity was not permitted by the jinn.

* * *

Finally, a few words must be said about stories of the jinn and individual dissimulation, or, simply put, faking it. I was warned repeatedly during the course of my research about sheikhs who are fakes, people who claim to be possessed who are fakes, and even about jinn who may fake an identity when they are in fact some other type of spirit. Veracity, it seems, is tricky in these matters. Yet villagers in Artas whom I spoke to about specific well-known cases, never called those who claimed to be afflicted liars. Some shrugged and replied to my queries about the women's stories noncommittally; others ventured explanations or additional details I had not heard.

One sheikh, however, with whom I spoke in Nablus when I accompanied a few villagers who were going to see him, told me the following story:

A man came to me. He said, "I have a daughter, the most beautiful of all the girls. Suddenly she has become like a mad woman. I brought you so that you will treat her." When we reached the house I asked about the girl and her father told me he locked her in a room in the house that had no windows. I went to the girl in this room. When I came in I found her sitting undressed with her hair unkempt. The girl asked me who I was. I said to her, "Don't say a word to me or I will turn you into a monkey! I am the king of the jinn! I came in order to solve your problems without anyone knowing. I will solve your problems if you just sit quietly. The first thing you must do is bathe, dress, and comb your hair and sit nicely. You are not crazy, you're just acting like it." I called her mother and told her mother to bring her clothes, bathe her, dress her, and comb her hair. Then I asked the girl what her problem was. We were alone. She said to me, "I love my *ibn khāl* [the son of her mother's brother]. My family wants to give me to my *ibn 'amm* [son of her father's brother]. I don't want my *ibn 'amm*. Because of this I am acting like I am crazy."

I told her, "Fine. I will solve your problems." Then I opened the door and asked her the name of her *ibn 'amm*. She told me his name and the name of her *ibn khāl*. I asked for her father and told him that her horoscope is connected to the horoscope of one of her relatives. I also said that when his daughter's *ibn 'amm* came to ask for her the jinn came to her and wore her. It is necessary, I said, to end the agreement between his daughter and her *ibn 'amm* and marry her to one with whom her horoscope agrees. Her *ibn 'amm* was standing there. I asked him, "Do you want the girl to be normal or do you want to marry her?" He said, "I don't want to marry her, I want her to be normal." After that they cancelled their agreement. Then I asked for twenty names from the names of the girl's relatives. The name of her *ibn khāl* was among these names. I said to them, "She is able to live with only one of these, her *ibn khāl*." They brought him and I asked him if he agreed to marry her. He agreed and the girl was very happy. Because I treated the girl, they slaughtered a sheep for me as a gift.

Here this sheikh, who has treated many Artasis, is admitting that the jinn may be used as a front, as a means of obtaining leeway in what may seem to be circumstances with no way out. The girl's explicit use of the jinn story removes the threat of marriage to her paternal cousin in favor of the marriage she desires to her maternal cousin. In this case the functionality of the jinn discourse is obvious. The story might be considered to be fraudulent because her possession episode was faked. The idea that a jinn may influence the course of events, however, remains.

A woman in her fifties in Artas told me the following story about her life, which I record here from my field notes:

After marrying her husband, she quickly realized his violent and unpredictable nature. He would beat her and their small children. He would go to Kuwait for ten months at a time to work, gamble away all his earnings, and then return home, worse than before he left. If it had not been for their ten children, six of whom were daughters, she would have left him for her natal family. But fearing for her children's future, she felt trapped into staying.

One day, desperate before his anticipated arrival from Kuwait, she went to a coffee cup reader. This reader told her that a man had come to her house to fix something and had spread magic all over the front porch. It was this magic that brought the jinn to her husband and caused her husband's violence. So she returned home and scrubbed the porch clean. When her husband returned home, he was a new man, a real human being, and all their problems were over.

When she finished this story, I asked her a few questions and she returned to her reminiscing:

She continued to recall the difficulties and pain of most of her married life. She told her story of her husband's departures and violent returns to and from Kuwait almost identically, but this time it had a slightly different ending: She

commented, "But from the day my husband got out of the Israeli prison, he was
a new man." Surprised, I reminded her of the magic, the coffee cup reader, and
the jinn. Clearly embarrassed, she reassured me, that, yes, she had also cleaned
the porch of the magic. Unable to go back at this point, however, she admitted
that the events had occurred in the following order: her visit to the coffee cup
reader and consequent cleansing of the evil magic and then her husband's release from prison (he had been arrested after his return from Kuwait).

This story may give voice to what should otherwise not be said: The Israeli
prison may have, in fact, changed her husband's violent nature for the better, perhaps making him grateful to return home. But who can admit that a husband's
trip to an Israeli prison can be beneficial for a wife? So the story of magic takes
precedence, until a slip of the tongue alerted both me and perhaps this woman to
the possibility that there are competing and, indeed, complementary explanations here, some of which may be too sensitive, or, at least unseemly, to be spoken of directly.

Finally, in a different incident, I was visited once in Artas by a young man
who claimed he could tell me everything I needed to know about the jinn,
"enough to write ten books," if I would simply pay him a rather hefty sum.
He had heard about me, he said, and simply wanted to help. To the horror of
my hosts, he had found his way to my home in the village by wandering along
the main village road asking where the foreigner was living. My hosts felt that
this public inquiry was embarrassing for me—and them. When he arrived,
only the children, the mother of my host family, and I were home. The father
of the family was out of the house. Hoping to avoid insulting the young man,
I simply said that I could not possibly make such a decision without "my uncle," the father of the family, present. He offered to demonstrate his ability to
summon a jinn and put anyone in the room into a trance; once again, I de-
murred, saying that my uncle would not approve of such things happening in
his home without his presence. The young man said he understood and left.

This visit became a source of many jokes between my hosts and me. We
assumed that the man was a fraud and that his intentions were less than honorable. Quite simply, none of us believed he had any particular talent or
knowledge about the jinn. Knowledgeable curers such as Ahmad or Im Musa
would never actively solicit business. Yet it was important to me to avoid outright offense; it was impossible to know if our paths would cross again, and
I did not want to risk alienating those who had stories to tell about the jinn
but had heard that I was in fact unsympathetic or uninterested in their experiences.

It was often important to villagers as well to avoid offending those who
claimed to be or to have been possessed, no matter how fraudulent their
claims might have seemed. Villagers were well aware that the intricacies of
village life demanded that one remain on good terms with everyone as of-

ten as possible. Calling individuals "liars" or "frauds" would not have been particularly tactful. Nonetheless, I do not want to suggest that all villagers shared equally in their beliefs about the jinn; rather, few shared with me explicit accusations that the women or, indeed, men who claimed to be afflicted by the jinn were lying. Certainly, many villagers had their doubts about some stories they would hear; I found the most typical response in those cases was the tactful comment that "only God knows." As for those who told me their own jinn stories, they often did so with a profound array of emotions. Aliyah, for example, whose prolonged experiences with the jinn are discussed in the following chapter, when speaking of the jinn, tried to hold back her tears as she talked of the jinn whom, she believes, has ruined her life. I understood her emotion to reflect her feelings about the seriousness and veracity of the matter for her.

In some cases (discussed in the next chapter) women troubled by the jinn believed they knew who had sent, via magical means, the jinn, and why. But I did not hear of a direct confrontation over such matters. This is certainly not to suggest that all kinds of confrontation are avoided in an effort to maintain harmonious relations (compare Wikan 1982). Indeed, loud fights among neighbors, between spouses, and even acquaintances, while not usually considered points of pride, are common. Rather, most people I know avoid confronting someone with a judgment on a matter that is best left to God to decide.

NOTES

1. Grace Crowfoot was an English woman who lived in the Middle East for many years in the early 1900s; she was very interested in botany and medicine as well as weaving and archaeological textiles. She was also a good friend of Louise Baldensperger. See Crowfoot and Baldensperger (1932).

2. Kahana found a similar origin tale (in this story Eve bore thirty, not forty, children) for the zar, a kind of jinn, among Christian Amhara and Jewish Falasha in Ethiopia (1985: 128).

3. In Morocco, Rosen (2002: 77–78) records a similar story of a jinn who guards treasure, hitting anyone who digs for it.

4. I did not hear stories relating the color of a jinn (or a jinn's clothing) to that jinn's identity, as are found in, for example, the Sudan (Boddy 1989: 187) and Amman (Khamal 1974, n.p.).

5. In Amman, the jinn have been described by Khamal (1974) as appearing in different color clothes, corresponding to their religious identity. A jinn who wears red clothes is an unbeliever, green clothes signify a Muslim jinn who is not very religious, and white clothes are worn by jinn who are both Muslim and religious; further, the jinn may appear in any shape, whether human or animal. As humans they are most easily recognized by their unusual, slanted and white eyes, feet which are similar to the hooves of donkeys, and particularly hairy bodies.

6. The unelaborated discourse of magic here is in contrast to cases in which the magic itself is oft-discussed and well known; compare Schmoll (1993), for example, on practices of soul-eating among the Hausa.

7. See, for example, Morsy (1991: 203) on treatment in Egypt.

8. Compare the role of the Islamic practitioner in Sudan, who treats certain cases of the jinn with the use of religious texts (Boddy 1989: 146); see also Lambek (1981) on Islamic fundis and cases of spirit possession in Mayotte.

9. Discussions of lifelong relations with spirits and their human hosts can be found in Ashkanani (1991: 224) on jinn in Kuwait; Boddy (1989: 142-145) on zar in Sudan; Lambek (1980: 319) on spirits in Madagascar.

10. Samaritans who live in and around Nablus are famous in the West Bank for their special abilities to treat the jinn. Indeed, I knew a few families in Artãs who made the long trip north to see these specialists. While they call themselves sheikhs, Samaritan specialists operate slightly differently from their Muslim counterparts. For example, they rely heavily on the use of horoscopes to determine the nature of a person's problem, instead of attempting to interact directly with the jinn. They consult literature not usually used by Muslim sheikhs and rely primarily on the use of written amulets.

11. Ashkanani similarly notes that in Kuwait in certain cases of possession, "it is more likely that the patient's family perceive her possession than that she sees it herself" (1991: 224).

12. Saleh (1975) describes variations of the mandal found in Jordan in the 1970s.

Chapter Three

Women and the Jinn

Told by and about Artasi women, the jinn stories in this chapter speak to issues that are painful and traumatic—spinsterhood, male emigration, moral transgressions, duplicity, and infertility—and that are often glossed over by villagers in the dominant discourses that speak of family unity, women's roles and responsibilities, and honor. The stories discussed here are distillations and compilations of many offhand references and informal discussions, as well as purposefully related narratives told by women about their own experiences while I was in Artas. Often, a woman or her close relatives would make reference to her jinn experience, and I would probe these casual remarks for more context and for the meaning the listeners and tellers found within the stories. Other times, a woman would share her story in detail and allow me to record it. These stories were told and heard against the backdrop of moral values which inform Artasis' daily lives. In what follows, I draw out my interpretations of these stories based on my understanding of broadly shared Artasi perspectives, values, and experiences, which I believe implicitly inform the stories' meanings.

NURA

Often jinn stories articulate the concerns and fears of family members and the unmarried women who cannot understand why they have been overlooked in the matchmaking processes. Amina, the sister of a young woman called Nura, told me the following story:

> Our aunt wanted Nura for her son, but Nura had decided to wait for another young man from the family [a distant relative] who was studying in America. This man had promised to come home to Palestine to marry her when he finished

his studies. So Nura's father told her aunt no. This was the beginning of the problem for Nura. After the family refused the aunt's request, the man in America decided to stay in America and marry. When other men came to meet Nura, after
the first meeting they never came back. We are all [Amina, her mother, and sis-
ters] convinced that our aunt made some kind of magic for Nura which brought
a jinn to her. This jinn frightens men away. Why else would Nura remain unmarried?

Nura was taken to numerous sheikhs to try to rid her of her jinn. Her aunt was
never directly confronted with the accusation that it was because of her that a
jinn troubled Nura. The jinn itself was decidedly unmarked; no one knew its
characteristics beyond the fact that it worked in subtle ways to prevent men
from asking to marry Nura. Nura herself would never discuss the topic with me,
but simply shrugged her shoulders and commented that "only God knows."
Amina and her female relatives, however, told this story over and over among
themselves, trying to figure out if anything else could be done to help Nura.
Nura is now thirty and teaches kindergarten in the village. Her story of the jinn
draws attention to a series of painful and problematic aspects of village life for
unmarried adult women, including problems posed by male emigration and the
relationships men leave behind; unmarried women's honorable reputations and
appropriate marriage age; education and its relationship to marriage prospects;
and the delicate balance between being unmarried and adult.

Male Emigration

Nura's story most immediately addresses the issue of male emigration and the
difficulties for young women who cannot leave the village themselves, but
must wait for those who have promised to return. The families of young men
who leave the village may promise that their sons will return but find that they
are unable to control their sons' actions once they are far away. Proximity, a
key factor in the social geography of village life, is an arm of control for parents over children, just as it is for neighbors over one another. When proximity is replaced by great distance, parental control lapses. Nura's relatives may
have wanted their son to return to marry Nura, but once in America, he chose
his own bride and later returned with her to Kuwait. In the meantime, Nura's
aunt may have sent Nura the jinn out of spite in the face of Nura's refusal to
marry her cousin, as Amina argues. This highlights additional problems posed
by emigration for those who do not leave the village: Will loved ones actually return? For how long and at what cost should villagers await their return?
Without daily upkeep, blood ties begin to lose meaning, and Nura's story
brings the villagers who ponder it uncomfortably close to realizing the pre-
cariousness of social ties strained by distance, whether those ties are between
parents and children, or a man and a woman he has promised to marry.

Nura's romantic hope of waiting for a young man who was studying in America and who promised to return for her further points to a social contradiction seldom discussed but increasingly influential with the younger generation: Romantic love, fostered by television soap operas, advertising images, and pop-Egyptian rock, no matter how appealing, is dangerous. Nura's aunt could have arranged for Nura's marriage with her son, a traditional cousin marriage. Nura, however, hoped for a more distant relative, an educated man who had lived and studied abroad. Hints of a brief romance between Nura and this young man surfaced now and then in our conversations about Nura and her jinn. Yet the lesson here is clear: romance, distance, and strangers—including kin who are far away—are risky at best, while closely located family members are real and fruitful supports.

Unmarried Adult Women

Nura's relatives, who tell and retell the story of Nura and her troubles with the jinn, draw attention away from Nura as a source of blame for remaining unmarried. Her relatives may be making a public bid for Nura's reinstatement in the community's "good book" by emphasizing the role of the jinn in conjunction with the potentially immoral role of Nura's aunt, who was bitter that Nura refused to marry her son.

Such a bid for honor is necessary because of the problematic state of a marriageable woman who remains unwed. Adult women who are married and young unmarried girls are the most commonly articulated "types" of women discussed publicly by villagers themselves. Significantly, in colloquial Arabic, *bint* refers to an unmarried and, therefore, virginal woman of any age, while *mar'a* refers to a woman who is married. I once mistakenly referred to a middle-aged woman as a *mar'a* and was quickly corrected that she, like the three year-old girl sitting on my lap at the time, was a *bint*, as she had never married. The distinction emphasized here and in general discussions is, obviously, that of marital status over age; thus the terms *bint* and *mar'a* do not correspond to the English words girl and woman respectively.

Nura's status challenges the well-established categories of young/unmarried and adult/married, by placing her as an unmarried yet clearly adult woman. Nura and other unmarried women find themselves out of place both symbolically as categorical misfits and literally as they are unable to maintain their own homes. Unable to enter fully into village life, there is no obvious geographical place for unmarried women, and they are thus largely without social standing. Indeed, perhaps the most problematic kind of marital status is that of an adult, healthy, morally upright woman who never marries, as opposed to one who is divorced or widowed. Divorce and remarriage is typical of a young woman whose first marriage lasted only briefly and who had no children by that marriage. In such cases, remarriage is quickly sought and often obtained by a woman's family. The same is generally true for young widows. But to remain unmarried is to call into question one's marriageable qualities—the quality of the girl's reputation being foremost among these qualities, and with her the quality of her family's reputation.

Villagers told me repeatedly that if a woman reaches twenty and has not yet married, her chances of marrying in the future become quite slim. These women are rarely publicly discussed, and their fate is understood to be undesirable and problematic. Unmarried grown women will live in their parents' houses until their parents die, and then usually live with a married sibling. They do not establish their own homes until they are quite elderly, if they do so at all. They care for their siblings' children and often work outside the home to bring home extra cash. These women are often but not always resented by their aging parents, who feel unduly burdened by the lifelong presence of an unmarried daughter in their home.

Nura's age alone—whether or not the jinn continues to afflict her—now makes the idea of finding a match unlikely. A man once commented to me that a girl should marry at fourteen when she is still "clean," in order to avoid becoming dirty, *wusikh*.[1] Here the suggestion is that as a girl becomes older, she risks accumulating hints of scandal or rumor to her reputation, thereby "dirtying" her.[2] A young girl has ideally spent most of her life in her family's home, supervised, untainted, unblemished, far from the public eye and far, therefore, from any risk of impropriety. Marriage at a young age insures that her reputation as a *bint* will remain perfect.

While marrying young may be one way for girls to remain "clean," marriage age also reflects to some extent the politics of occupation: One study has shown a rise in early marriage (marriage below the age of eighteen) in the Bethlehem and Tulkarim districts in 1988–1989, the years immediately following the outbreak of the first intifada. Possible reasons for this increase include extended school closures (making it nonsensical to delay marriage for girls until after their schooling), difficult economic circumstances (making it difficult for households to take care of all their members and thus inclined to encourage marriage for their girls as an economic measure), cheaper weddings during this time (the Unified Leadership banned wedding parties during the intifada), and a "psychological dimension at play in which death is considered even more tragic for a young man if he leaves no male heir behind" (cited by Hammami 1994: 288-89). It remains to be seen how the possibility of peace or continued crisis will affect the marriage age for women. Marriage age is also affected by a range of structural changes in Palestinian society, including changes in education and work opportunities (see Hammami 1994: 291) as well as moral evaluations of women's appropriate roles and needed skills in village life.

Nura would have been in her early twenties during the first intifada, already on the older side of the spectrum for marriageable girls. In retrospect, it is difficult to know how the intifada affected her opportunities for marriage. Yet it is clear to Nura's sisters and immediate family that the jinn affected her, and that this jinn was quite possibly related to a number of other factors at work in village life.

Education

One common practice that is intended to help assure that young unmarried girls remain "clean" and desirable as prospective wives with unblemished reputations is to stop schooling girls at a young age.[3] Here it is important to know that Nura finished teacher's college training to become a kindergarten teacher. Many young women, in contrast, drop out soon after age fourteen, the acceptable age for marriage. Only a few girls every year from Artas finish the final three years of secondary school in Bethlehem (at the time of my fieldwork the Artas girls' school contained only the first nine grades).[4] If girls do finish secondary school, complete the *tawjihi* exam (the General Secondary Education Certificate Examination), and go on to secretarial or teacher training programs or university, many feel they risk dirtying their reputations by being seen coming and going from the village in the cars that run between Artas and Bethlehem or, even worse, by walking, if they cannot afford the fare. Most young women recognize that this option seriously jeopardizes their chances for marriage. While few girls want to take such a risk with their future and thus drop out of school willingly to await marriage, others claim that their families do not give them the choice of continuing in school. Based on the 1992 FAFO survey, Heiberg (1994: 138) reports that 37 percent of Palestinian women between the ages of 15 and 19 years old have left school with nine years or less of education; 28 percent of this group reported the reason for leaving school as marriage.

Nura's jinn takes the blame for her unmarried status, removing her educational background from direct blame. Yet in the context of village life, we are led to wonder about the relationship between the educated woman, her jinn, and unmarried status—and the implicit critique Nura's story thus contains of some of the potential consequences of education for a woman. A more explicit critique was offered to me by one young woman, Nisreen, who told me the following when asked questions about schooling for girls in Artas:

> We have for our girls traditions and practices; I mean, the girls stay in the house with their families and don't go outside of the house. I mean, she goes and comes but not far from her family. If the girl today goes out of the house, she will ask her father and tell him the place that she is going to go. Our girls get married young. There are a lot of girls who leave school and don't continue their studies. I mean, they are ignorant. As for Israel, the first thing they do is give freedom [*ḥurrīya*] to the girl, she gos and comes. With respect to them this is normal. They don't ask their family. This is something not good. Because if the girl goes out from the house her family does not know maybe if she went out with a boy.

This is how one loses her *sharaf* [honor]. The girl in Israel, also she does not marry early, I mean, any time she wants, she marries. The girl finishes her education in Israel. But us, we don't have girls who finish their education. Not all, of course. There are some people who let their girls complete their studies.

These comments further reflect on the degree to which Israeli cultural practices as understood by Artasis have infiltrated villagers' awareness. While largely rejected, Israeli practices provide a mirror that village women may use to measure themselves more clearly. Indeed, many young girls in the village also commented to me that they would have liked to stay in school longer. They may have felt they had to say that to me in light of the fact that, to them, it seemed I had stayed in school far too long (and, indeed, at the time of my fieldwork, I was unmarried). But it is equally possible that they did want to stay in school or that they felt ambivalent about the decision to leave school. Nisreen's comments here on the common village practice of removing girls from school when they are young are, at least in part, unflattering. Indeed, she points out, even a few people in the village allow girls to finish their studies, or, in other words, even a few villagers recognize the value of a girl's education and presumably hope that such an education will not jeopardize her future happiness.

Unmarried and Adult

Nura's story of the jinn further leads us to reflect on how she is caught between two contradictory dictates for achieving social standing for an unmarried woman who is an adult: She must balance the restrictions pertinent to the lives of young unmarried women while contributing productively to the work of the household, as she is an adult consumer of its goods. While each family decides for itself the rules for its young unmarried girls, there are some widely shared practices and perspectives that often structure these girls' lives and to which Nura must remain attuned, although she cannot abide entirely by them, regardless of whether or not she desires to do so. Such practices include limiting one's visibility to other village acquaintances (e.g., remaining at home or in the immediate vicinity, doing little of the household work that takes her out of the home, etc.).

Yet Nura cannot remain in her family's home or even the immediate neighborhood everyday. She must answer to the pragmatic demand that, as an adult woman, she contribute to the household work. As a contributor to the *shughl*, she needs to engage in activities that make her highly visible, such as doing the shopping when other family members—the married women and men of the household—are too busy to do it. She should and does in her work as a teacher also contribute to the household income, a duty that further complicates the issue of her femininity, as it is ideally men who should work for a wage outside the home.

It is interesting to note that Nura was the only woman I met in Artas who had a driver's license. Her established adult, single status meant that the criticism this would entail for a younger, unmarried, but still eligible woman, was largely meaningless. In the first few months of my fieldwork I was often asked if I had a driver's license and was initially puzzled by the significant surprise that accompanied my affirmative answer; clearly, possessing a driver's license was another sign of my problematic status and a possible symbol of my lack of respectability. While Nura certainly did not achieve the status of an "honorary man" in village life, she nonetheless experienced a complicated mix of restrictions, obligations, and opportunities, if at a significant cost.

Nura herself remains quiet and unheard, perhaps in part due to the nature of her character, as well as her attempts to meet the demands that she must try to be rarely visible and rarely talked about by others, to maintain a clean reputation. Ironically, necessity forces her to be seen in highly visible spaces, and her own loved ones talk about her plight often and in detail.

HALAH

Halah, unlike Nura, was willing to discuss her own experience of being unmarried and troubled by the jinn, as well as to hypothesize how these two states came to be. Halah, like Nura, now works for a wage. She was trained by nuns in Bethlehem to do *tatriz*, or the cross-stitch embroidery that adorns many women's dresses, pillows, and other decorative items. Many young women who are unmarried and no longer attending school participate in programs that train them to sew or embroider, skills they may use on a part-time basis at home after they marry. When I asked Halah to tell me about her experiences with the jinn, she began with the following:

> My two oldest brothers, one was in Saudi and one was in Libya. They used to stay out of the country, and their wives stayed here [the two brothers married two sisters from Artas]. I and my sister were like servants for them. We would do their laundry, prepare everything for them, cooking. And they would sleep or go on trips, or eat sunflower seeds. All of the work was my and my sister's responsibility. After a while my sister married and I stayed alone. I said to myself, I am going to be a servant for my brother's wives whenever they come here. I began to stay away from them, to stop visiting them. Eventually my two brothers came back here and now have their own homes. I don't visit them because I don't want to be their servant. I stopped helping them. I slowly stopped visiting or helping them completely. When I stopped helping them, they threw me away and stopped taking care of me, as if I am garbage.
>
> Slowly, slowly grooms began to come and ask for my hand. Whenever a groom would come to ask for my hand, my father would refuse and give any excuse, that the groom was too young, or too old, too thin, too dark, too poor.

Whenever a groom would come my father would always have an excuse for not accepting him. Sometimes, my father would tell me that I am his legs and hands and he can't get rid of those. One day, Mahmoud [a man from Artas] asked for my hand. I came to my brother and started pulling my hair and saying, "Please, let my father agree." But my brother said, "Your father disagreed and I can't do anything." He said, "My father is older and knows better; he is the one who has to say first whether or not he agrees, and then I would say if I agree or not." So my brother said that he couldn't disobey my father. So then my brother went to Mahmoud's house and told them that my father didn't agree.

One day, my brother said that he wanted to know why my father is against me getting married. My brother took me and Aliyah to a place in Jerusalem. We sat with a sheikh who was holding a book. And I couldn't understand anything in the book. You can't understand anything from what is written. It had no punctuation. Then the sheikh told me, without me telling him anything, the names of the people who came to ask for my hand. He began to tell me that I feel pain sometimes in my head, eyes, or right hand and that I live in bad conditions. It was like he knew every single thing about my life without me telling him anything. He began to put his hand on my head and read Qu'ran. Sometimes he put his hand on my chest, or my legs, and continue reading. Then my brother asked the sheikh to tell us the problem and what he found, if there was any magic done to me. The sheikh said, Someone did magic to her seven years ago and now she has a jinn who troubles her. We went to this sheikh three years ago, so now the magic has been done to me for ten years. My brother paid 300 shekels to the sheikh so he would get rid of the magic and the jinn, but he couldn't. The sheikh said that the magic is buried under the wastes of animals [magic is often written on a small piece of paper] and it is very difficult to find, and it is not easy to rip up. So then my brother told me that I have to be patient and that I must read the Qu'ran.

According to the sheikh, he said that one of the people closest to me did the magic. Because of that, you can see that I am very skinny, short, and not married. And I am always distracted. Until now, my brothers' wives treat me like garbage. My life is getting worse every day. My family used to say to me that no one would come to ask for my hand. But when people did come to ask for my hand, my family used to say to me that the moment they looked at my face they fled. They say these things to make up excuses for why I am not married, so I feel that it is my mistake and not theirs. Now I am sure that the magic which is done to me is from them. But now the sheikh wants 300 JDs [Jordanian dinars] in order to get rid of this magic. He told to me that if I brought him 300 JDs he would tell me exactly who did this to me and he would get rid of it. But from where can I bring 300 JDs? I have a problem with my hand now and all my money now goes to treat my hand. My brother helped me to do the operation for my hand, but still.

Halah's experience of magic and the jinn shares many of the themes explored in Nura's story. Perhaps most importantly, the jinn in Halah's life, as in Nura's, takes the blame for Halah's unmarried status, removing her from blame and holding out the possibility that Halah herself has done nothing "wrong" that could have damaged her reputation and made her an undesirable prospect as a wife. Blaming Halah herself is thus unfair to her and her attempts to maintain her honorable reputation: The presence of the jinn is proof that we should not blame Halah.

Further, Halah's experience speaks to believing that those to whom one is closest can also be the most dangerous. As in Nura's case, a close relative was suspected of having sent the jinn with its deleterious consequences, although Halah's suspicions were confirmed by a sheikh. For Halah, however, her father also complicates matters, for he is too selfish to think of what is best for her future, instead of his own need for her help. Her brothers' wives also prove to be self-centered, appreciating Halah only when she does their housework and otherwise believing her to be useless. The strain of this work for Halah and her family members' ingratitude highlights the domestic work often required of unmarried adult women and its difficulty. This work does not directly benefit these women in the ways that a married woman's work in her own home and with her own children benefits her: Halah gains little status or respect for this work but must do it as she is a member of the household with no home of her own to take care of or provide an excuse for her not to work for others. Halah longs for marriage and the opportunity to establish her own household.

Halah's eventual refusal to perform household labor for her sisters-in-law in particular may well be related to the advent of the jinn in her life, although the specific doer of the magic which brought the jinn remains unknown. Whether wrought by her father or the sisters-in-law for whom she has worked so hard, these duplicitous actions on the part of some of Halah's closest relatives further demonstrate the danger inherent in "close" relations, a closeness that optimally protects and supports an individual, but may also oppress and threaten her. Halah is keenly aware of her family's attempts to blame her for her misfortune and to ignore the role they have played in creating her problematic situation. "They say these things to make up excuses for why I am not married, so I feel that it is my mistake and not theirs," Halah says. But she knows her troubles can be traced to a jinn brought by one of them.

Halah's father is well-known for his domineering personality in the village. Even Halah's older brother is powerless before his father's refusal to allow Halah to marry and the jinn's influence. Halah, for her part, may refuse to do housework for her sisters-in-law, but must continue to do the work in her father's house. Visiting sheikhs and enlisting the help of her brother are her only paths for attempting to change her situation. Yet even here she is stymied because she cannot pay the sheikh the amount of money he requires to finally rid her of the magic, and her brother advises her only to read the Qu'ran, although she is largely illiterate.

SARA

Sara is a young woman whom I met only briefly. I accompanied her father, Ahmad, to Nablus to visit the sheikha described in chapter 2. In the car on the way to Nablus, Ahmad showed us two photos of his daughter that told of her (in his view) social demise. The first picture was taken on her engagement day, when Sara was "wearing" a pink, frilly dress and a lot of gold jewelry. Sara was her father's vision of respectable femininity in this photo—engaged, dressed in a pink dress, and displaying jewelry from her groom. In the second photo she was sitting on a park bench, in jeans and a t-shirt, with a headscarf on her head—a picture of troublesome feminism. Ahmad explained that his daughter had been engaged but inexplicably changed her mind and could not be persuaded to reaccept. Since then, not a single young man had come to ask for her hand. At the time of our trip to Nablus, Sara was sixteen. Ahmad was concerned about the fate of his daughter and deeply worried that she would end up unmarried. Convinced that someone had sent Sara a jinn who first made her change her mind about marrying and then kept eligible men away from her, Ahmad decided to see the sheikha in Nablus and ask for her help. He then asked me not to mention his trip to Nablus to his daughter. Ahmad's story of Sara's jinn adds an important dimension of what these issues look like from the point of view of a concerned father.

The fast-paced social changes and the increasing range of opportunities for young women in village life are clear here. Sara wants something besides early marriage, while Ahmad's actions speak of a father's fears for his daughter, his fear that she will end up without a "place" in village life. Her story further speaks to her father's inability to comprehend that she may not want to get married for any number of reasons; he can see only that she must, and he is willing to enlist the help of a sheikha in order to redress any supernatural barriers that may exist.

By articulating his concerns for his daughter in terms of the jinn, Ahmad is removing her from direct blame, as in the cases of Nura and Halah. Far from feeling that he must force her into marriage, Ahmad instead expressed his fear for her well-being and future happiness if she does not marry quickly, before she becomes too old to be considered a good prospect. The source of blame for such a predicament would not rest with his honorable daughter, but rather with the jealousy and envy of others who want to deny her happiness. The need for Sara to marry, or, at least to be found to be afflicted by the jinn if she does not, is overwhelming. Sara's father admitted that he was desperate for her to marry, but at least to know that a jinn was responsible for her not marrying. The overwhelming pressure to marry is clear in this story; the consequences of not marrying are high, pointing to the power of this life cycle prerequisite.

THE JINN AND
THE VIRGIN GIRL

Sharaf al-bint, a girl's honor, is largely dependent upon her lack of public visibility and the limited *hurrīya* structuring an adolescent girl's life that ensures
she will remain a virgin until her marriage. For an unmarried girl to lose her
virginity in the village is an action that, it is well known, will have dire consequences for her and her family. In some cases, it is said, such a girl should
be murdered in an "honor killing," or married off to a far-away old man. Men's
and women's discussions of this kind of moral mistake on the part of the
young girl and the consequences she can expect to suffer never varied in daily
conversation. Although such incidents were reported in other parts of the West
Bank (see Ruggi 1998, Rubenberg 2001: 44-7), no villager could tell me of a
recent case of an honor killing of a young girl in Artas. After acknowledging
that no honor killing had taken place in recent memory, every villager with
whom I spoke nonetheless affirmed that this punishment would be carried out
if necessary.

Yet I recorded one story of the jinn that explicitly suggests that villagers
may prefer a far different course of action in practice. A girl "on the other side
of the village" (no matter who told this story the girl was always "on the other
side of the village") was about thirteen or fourteen when a jinn came to her
and possessed her. This jinn caused her to lose her virginity by the act of possessing her. Her family attempted to have her treated by various sheikhs.
Eventually, an elderly villager who deals in the *mandal* entered into negotiations with the jinn and persuaded him to leave the girl. The girl was then in
good health. Not long afterwards she married her first cousin (her father's
brother's son) and is now happy.

This tale of possession by the jinn suggests a course of action radically different from honor killings or banishment. Not only does the girl marry, but she
does so to a desirable mate, her paternal first cousin. Importantly, the girl is not
being held responsible for the possession or its (otherwise dire) consequences;
in daily life, by contrast, should a girl elicit attention from men on the street,
for example, she is generally believed to be the one who is in the wrong. This
story of the jinn and a young girl's loss of her virginity recasts blame onto the
jinn and allows the girl to continue in good standing in the eyes of her family
and community. Here the powerful demand that a young girl be a virgin at
marriage is simply foregone, in light of the jinn's interference.

While villagers will tout a distinct and strict moral line delineating the appropriate behavior of women in particular and punishment for those women
who cross that line, in practice mistakes in judgment are often minimized and
covered up. This jinn story powerfully voices this practice of "cover-up" of
an obvious subversion of the moral code. The incidents that may be covered

up range from a young girl illicitly kissing a boy, to a husband who beats his wife. This particular tale of the jinn may seem surprisingly forgiving in its tone: the girl's family believed her story of possession, had her treated appropriately, and then married her to a cousin, one who should have her best interests at heart. It is a story of a daughter's good treatment at the hands of her family. But it is also more than that. The story's focal point—the loss of the girl's virginity—is an unthinkable offense to the rules of proper social behavior for young unmarried women. By emphasizing her family's moderation, the story articulates a radically different view of the village social world from the one formally articulated in both men's and women's discourse. This story shows a social world in which the problems, misguided behaviors, and mistakes of individuals are indeed "covered-up"—minimized, forgiven, and forgotten in practice.

This story has echoes in an incident that occurred while I was in Artas. 'Abd, a young man who had recently come from Amman, caught one of his young female relatives kissing a boy behind a house. He told the girl's aunt. The aunt scolded 'Abd for spreading rumors and attempting to create problems where there were none. The young cousin's movements, I noticed, were increasingly circumscribed after the event, but nothing more came of the incident.

Virginity is certainly touted as a young bride's most important quality. Traditional demands for demonstrating the virginity of the bride upon her wedding night by producing a bloodied cloth is handled on a case-to-case basis, however, and may reflect a certain practical approach to the issue. If a man has married a stranger bride, for example, the groom's mother may request to see the sheet stained with blood following the wedding night. The sheet or any other proof of evidence of the bride's virginity will not, in any case, be shown publicly. In general, however, if a man has married a relative from the village no such request is made. It is often rumored that intercourse may not take place on the first night of the marriage in any case, and evidence of a bride's virginity may be a long time coming. For people who have known a young girl and her family their entire lives, asking for proof of her virginity is nothing less than an insult. Surely they are familiar enough with the quality of the girl and her family not to doubt the girl's untarnished reputation. However, following the couple's first night together, the bride's washed undergarments and nightclothes will often be hung out to dry in front of the home for all to see. Without any other laundry, the message of the clothes on the front laundry lines is clear: the new bride inside the house is now a married woman.

This story of a young girl's loss of virginity to a jinn comments on the moral person's ability to overlook, pretend to not see, or simply to reinterpret certain publicly known acts that could incriminate an individual. The dominant discourse of honor and the stated rules for punishment of those who do not adhere to it are temporarily subverted. The honor code carries consequences for the guilty parties that are known in some cases to be simply too high. This story directs our attention to a fault line, a space in the hegemonic social order, a space that allows socially wise adults *not* to practice what are stated as "the rules." This exception speaks to the unspoken in the public performance of (im)morality: there are events which should not be accepted as they are actually known—even if carried out in a public manner—for fear of their repercussions.

ALIYAH

Stories of the jinn do not address only the concerns and experiences of unmarried women. Women who experience infertility also often have jinn stories to tell; I explore two such stories here. Aliyah was one of my closest friends in Artas. We shared being in difficult social positions in the village—she was married but childless, and I was the neighborhood anthropologist, old enough to be married but single, American, and of Jewish background. We were also the same age, a fact we examined and considered often as we discussed our lives. Aliyah left school when she was twelve and was married at the age of fourteen. In Artas I lived in a home directly next to the home of Aliya and her husband (in actuality, physically below their home, so that her front porch was level with my family's second floor bedroom balcony and overlooked our main living rooms). During my first night in Artas, the eldest daughter of the family with whom I lived systematically told me about all the neighbors, beginning with Aliyah and the fact of her childlessness. Aliyah and I became close friends in the months that followed and I slowly learned about her and her life.

By the time I arrived in Artas, Aliyah and her husband had already struggled with infertility for years and had visited numerous sheikhs in Bethlehem and Jerusalem in an attempt to fathom what kind and how many jinn might be troubling Aliyah to the point that she could not conceive. Aliyah told me that she and her husband were also trying to learn who had sent the jinn to Aliyah, and why. So sheikh after sheikh attempted to "speak" to Aliyah's jinn, or put Aliyah into a trance so her jinn might speak through her. Yet neither strategy worked—Aliyah's jinn could not be summoned.

The sheikhs then prescribed amulets; some were to be worn around Aliyah's neck, others placed under her pillow while she slept, and so on. The amulets were intended to ward off the jinn who plagued Aliyah and kept her from conceiving. Lambek argues that "wearing Koranic verses and astrological symbols sewn into amulets and tied around the neck or waist forms a kind of continuous 'illocutionary' act [illocutionary acts include blessings, oaths, protections, and sanctifications of the events that follow] . . . the amulets provide an ongoing declaration of commitment, a fusion of statement and state"

(1990: 27). Wearing an amulet is thus similar to saying the proper blessings before performing certain acts; as discussed in chapter 2, when a person forgets to recite a blessing, the jinn may attack. Thus Aliyah's amulets were meant to act as a constant source of protection for her.

Eventually, the sheikhs became too expensive and the effort too great for Aliyah and her husband to continue to visit them. When their visits to the sheikhs finally stopped completely, Aliyah became increasingly depressed and socially isolated. Unwilling to go out and visit her neighbors or relatives for fear of what people would say about her, Aliyah rarely left her house. Her sisters and female neighbors were busy with their young children and rarely visited.

While I was in Artas, Aliyah and her husband visited medical specialists who identified the problem as being in large part her husband's. Subsequently, an *in vitro* fertilization attempt at a clinic in Nablus failed. Aliyah firmly believes now that, in addition to her husband's medical problem, she was long ago cursed to be followed by a jinn, not actually possessed by it, but in a sense, "haunted" by its presence so that she cannot become pregnant. For months I tried to persuade Aliyah to tell me who she believed had sent this jinn to her, but she refused. Only toward the end of my fieldwork did Aliyah finally suggest that the person who had sent the jinn to her was someone to whom she was "close," and someone who harbored jealous resentment of her, but she refused to be more specific.

SA'IDA

A woman in her earlier thirties, whom I call Sa'ida here, told me that she and her first husband were unable to have children. Sa'ida's experience with the jinn, in contrast to Aliyah's, was vivid and painful. From the day she married, Sa'ida claimed to have had a headache. After about a year of marriage, a sheikh was brought to the house because Sa'ida had begun to scream and flail about uncontrollably. My research assistant and his family witnessed this episode and described it to me repeatedly during my time in the village. The sheikh read the Qu'ran over Sa'ida for two hours while her family held her still. She eventually calmed, the jinn left her, and the sheikh pronounced her cured. She was convinced that she experienced childlessness because her husband's family did not like her, and that one among them had made some kind of magic to bring a jinn to her to prevent her from getting pregnant. This jinn would come to her in a dream and hit her in her stomach. The morning following her dream, she always got her period. When she and her first husband divorced, the jinn stopped bothering her. She has now remarried but she still does not have children.

Infertility

Although the nature of their interactions with the jinn differed significantly, Aliyah and Sa'ida's stories of the jinn do share some characteristics. Both women experienced infertility for a period of time with dire consequences in terms of their social standing in the village. Aliyah had slowly become imprisoned in her house, a hostage to public opinion, and depressed; Sa'ida suffered similarly, refusing to go to family gatherings or village weddings. Both also suffered severe criticism and, at times, social ostracism. Infertility is a deeply problematic experience for both women and men, although women are more vulnerable than men to charges that they are at fault in such matters.

Their narrations also blame the jinn for their infertility, a fact which helped these two women considerably. Both Aliyah and Sa'ida directed attention away from themselves as "failures" by locating the source of their infertility in the jinn. Here Boddy's argument about the relationship between possession and infertility in Sudan is particularly apt:

> It is not because fertility dysfunction is in her 'nature,' and not necessarily because it was foreordained by Allah, that she suffers. Possession, in fact asserts the opposite: that she is fertile, for spirits have usurped this asset in a bid to attain their selfish ends. Thus it rationalizes the untoward event in a way which vehemently defends and absolves the socialized self. (Boddy 1989: 188)

Further:

> Zar illness contains an oblique admission that fertility, though socially regulated and vested in women, is not humanly governable, for beings more powerful than Hofriyati may intervene at will to obstruct its proper course. (Boddy 1989: 188)

Aliyah's and Sa'ida's jinn stories provide a means for discussing their concerns about infertility and redirecting blame for their infertility onto the jinn. In Aliyah's case, by presuming the jinn were at fault, blame was cast outside of Aliyah and her husband, which may have contributed to the preservation of their marriage by lessening the pressure to dissolve it from either Aliyah's or her husband's family (divorce is a common course of action in childless marriages). Aliyah's story may also have been an implicit acknowledgment that her husband could be to blame physically for their childlessness. For Sa'ida, blame was similarly redirected onto the jinn, but in this case such a focus may have allowed her not only to be divorced but also to remarry without undue concern that the fault for the infertility was solely hers.

The social dynamics in which the two women are enmeshed—dynamics that in this case insist on the responsibility of a married woman to be fertile—are mystified or hidden. Indeed, neither woman explicitly questioned or challenged the moral mandate of fertility. Having a large family is the goal of most of the young women I knew in Artas. I also knew a few young women who suggested to me that they certainly wanted children, but not too many, and not too close together. Rhoda Kanaaneh has persuasively argued that Palestinians in the Galilee "increasingly define themselves in terms of fertility and use reproductive control as a measure of modernity—or, alternatively, Arab authenticity" (2002: 255). For Palestinians in the West Bank and Gaza she suggests that the "counter-discourse," a discourse emphasizing a "romanticized traditionalism" and opposing Israeli population policy control measures, is "likely to be even more pronounced after years of Israeli military occupation" (2002: 255). This reasoning may well be true, particularly in light of the criticisms Artasi women voice about their Israeli counterparts' moral practices. Yet when a woman in Artas is believed to be using birth control, the criticism most often voiced by other women is that she is doing something hidden, secret, and, therefore, most likely immoral. A woman should not have secrets. She should have nothing to hide. Her external appearance is the truest accounting of her "self." Women who go for years without being visibly pregnant are morally suspect.

Women who want children but are unable to conceive are thus in the problematic position of not being able to demonstrate their fertility; they further lack the amount of housework which would allow them to show the extent of their cleanliness. A woman who has few or no children has little *shughl*, daily housekeeping work, and is likely to be criticized as lazy, quite possibly immoral, and lacking the children who would (and should) create her most meaningful source of work. Infertile married women thus lack the basic requirements needed to establish themselves as respectable, mature women. By identifying the jinn rather than themselves as responsible, the public censure which accompanies Aliyah's and Sa'ida's "failure" to conform was lessened (for Aliyah, by allowing the marriage to go on, which is what she wanted) and, even, reversed (for Sa'ida, by allowing her to remarry).

Close Relations

By understanding the jinn as sent by someone close to them, both Aliyah and Sa'ida are led to the conclusion that contained within those close relationships is the source of their problem with the jinn, and that someone close sent the jinn to prevent their ability to conceive. The motivations of the jinn are equated here with the desire of a human individual to send the jinn to her neighbor or kinswoman. When Aliyah and Sa'ida recount their experiences with the jinn (and others retell the two women's stories), similar to Nura and Halah's stories of the jinn, they are articulating an aspect of the ambiguity that inheres in "close" relations. One should be and feel close to both one's neighbors and family. Yet, in practice, these close relationships, even when carefully chosen and fostered, are often threatened by deceit, unknown resentments, or evil intentions.

By believing that those to whom they are "close" sent a jinn to prevent them from bearing children, Sa'ida and Aliyah are expressing fear of the power that those to whom they are close can exercise over their lives. Aliyah and Sa'ida suffer daily the repercussions of not having children: public censure, vicious gossip, and their own diminished feelings of self-worth. By identifying their "close ones" as those who created the pretext and context for their suffering, Aliyah and Sa'ida are suggesting the unpredictable and potentially dangerous nature of kin and/or neighborly ties. They are implicitly saying: "You may not only dislike or be disliked by those to whom you are close, you may also find that they can boldly damage you and your reputation." The implication that a relative sent the jinn may or may not be acknowledged in cases of possession, but the fact that it is a possibility directs our attention to a woman's social network and the roles played by that network in her life.

This experience of the demonstrable power of close relations (kin or neighbors) for Aliyah and Sa'ida adds a significant dimension to the discussion of the nature of family. While one may choose those to whom one is close based on personal preference and maintain those relations through the practices of neighborliness, those relationships may be as dangerous as relationships that are left unfostered. Here the "kind of family that matters" acquires a more cynical layer of meaning: for a young married woman childless after a year of marriage, the "kind of family that matters" may be those who surround you and who are able most easily to threaten your happiness.

However, by refusing to reveal more specifically the identity of those whom they suspect of having sent them the jinn, Aliyah and Sa'ida are able to continue to interact with those to whom they are close. As Lambek argues for the occurrence of sorcery in Mayotte:

The frequent occurrence of sorcery does not cause social ruptures and realignments of the sort, and to the degree, described for other African societies. Rather, the experience of sorcery leads to a painful awareness of the discrepancy between public norms and private sentiments. (1981: 45)

Aliyah's and Sa'ida's "painful awareness" of deception remains tacit and unarticulated. They are able, therefore—indeed, are forced by the social mores of politeness—to continue to interact with those around them despite their misgivings. The relationships are preserved in large part due to the inability to know with precision exactly who is responsible for the jinn's influence from a large network of close relatives and neighbors.

There is a fourth strand to be followed in the cases of Aliyah and Sa'ida. This strand involves the responses of their husbands to their beliefs that they are troubled by the influence of a jinn. In Sa'ida's case, her husband divorced her shortly after her most vivid experience of possession. In Aliyah's case, her husband slowly investigated other possibilities for treatment until he found the fertility clinic in Nablus. Both men were moved to take action of a rather extreme kind by village standards. Divorce in Artas is relatively rare; women like Sa'ida typically do not initiate the process. Aliyah had never travelled beyond Bethlehem. Finding the clinic, traveling to and from Artas and Nablus, and receiving in vitro fertilization treatments were beyond her abilities to arrange or to finance by herself. In these incidents, we see that the incidents of spirit possession provided a necessary impetus—and justification—for the two men's actions.

While no relationship between the jinn and the husbands developed in these cases, it may nonetheless be useful to interpret these incidents of possession as offering heightened opportunities for communication between husband and wife. "Possession operates to transmit messages (verbal, material, etc.) between senders and receivers along particular channels" (Lambek 1981: 70). Neither Aliyah nor Sa'ida could have demanded expensive trips to a fertility specialist or divorce (respectively) without risking their reputations or their families' wrath. Neither woman may have had these particular outcomes in mind, as a each woman slowly became convinced that she was troubled by a vengeful jinn. Rather, Sa'ida's final dramatic episode and Aliyah's slow loss of hope demonstrated to their husbands the seriousness of the problem and that something had to be done. The two husbands arrived at dramatically different conclusions, but both were spurred to take action by the power of their wives' jinn.

SAMIRA

Samira, a married woman in her thirties, told me the following:

> I was feeling ill, like there was something pushing on my chest. I went to doctors but they could not help. So I went to an Arabic doctor [a sheikh]. He asked me, "What do you really feel?" While he asked, he was holding and looking at the Qu'ran. "What's bothering you? What's the matter?" I said, "I feel like there's a struggle inside of me, like there's something trying to choke me." The sheikh said, "You have a balcony in your house and it does not have tile. One day you brought water and spilled it without saying the name of Allah. So when you spilt the water there was a jinn in that place who was the son of a king. He is a Muslim jinn, not Christian or Jewish. The jinn hit you because he wants to marry you. Did you see the jinn in your dreams? Can you see him in any way? Did he try to attack or disturb you?" I answered, "When I take a bath on Fridays and put on makeup, he tries to hurt me and choke me. But he feels mercy for me, so he does not hurt me. Also, he does not hurt me because he wants to marry me."
>
> Once my son Mahmoud was sleeping, when he was very little. My son told his father that he saw a very tall man next to the wall trying to choke me. After Mahmoud told my husband this, then I saw something, something very tall, and his hands were very long, something like a shadow and he was trying to choke me,

but I pushed his hands away from my neck. After that I had a pain in my hands for nearly a month. I began screaming and I grabbed my husband's neck and began crying and asking him to save me from the jinn. My husband went and called his brother and they began to read the Qu'ran over me. They brought the Qu'ran and put it under my head. They started to read the Qu'ran and the shadow began to leave the house. When the shadow was next to the door it began to burn from the ground to the sky. After that everything was back to normal. If my son had not seen the jinn and warned me that he was coming to choke me, maybe I would be dead now. I don't know why he wanted to marry me. He's the son of a king, too good for me, and I'm married, but it doesn't matter to him if I'm married or not.

When I wore the jinn, he particularly bothered me when I had my period because I was unclean. Especially also when I took a bath and put on makeup he bothered me too. So the sheikh advised me not to put on makeup. The jinn are really made from fire. The jinn was really sweet to me because he loved me so much! I was thinner than you and prettier, but now I have too many children. A man can be close to Allah because he goes to work in the morning, returns in the evening and has time to read the Qu'ran. But women are always in the house, doing the work, taking care of the kids. There's always something to do. We don't have time to be close to Allah or pray or read the Qu'ran. Always the man can read the Qu'ran. That's why the jinn always wear the women.

Samira's involvement with the jinn began, according to the sheikh, because she spilled water without saying the name of Allah, a relatively common offense (as discussed in chapter 2). This offense gave the jinn the opportunity to bother her, which it did, according to the sheikh and Samira, because the jinn wanted to marry Samira. We are given little description of the jinn. We know only that he appeared as a shadow—tall, and with strong hands. Embedded in Samira's narrative is the identification of particular moments when she feels herself to be at moral risk, as well as commentary on the difficult nature of women's work within marriage.

Moments of Risk

Samira specifically identifies having her period with not being clean—a clear opportunity for the jinn to attack her. In many of the stories I gathered from sheikhs and villagers, women suffer from attacks by the jinn when they are having their periods. Menstruation is rarely, if ever, discussed in normal conversation. Yet, in large (and mixed-sex) settings, the fact that a woman was menstruating and consequently "not clean" while attacked by the jinn was spoken of matter-of-factly.

In moments when Samira is fostering her cleanliness and beauty, however—bathing and putting on makeup, particularly—she is also at risk from the jinn. Bathing and wearing makeup are generally thought of as important for a woman's sense of self-esteem in a public setting, such as a wedding. Indeed, Samira's description of the jinn's love for her contains within it a sense of pride in herself and her appearance, at least before having her children. Many of the young married women I knew were careful to look their best when able to be seen by others. Most young married women, for example, put on lipstick even when walking to the spring to bring water back to their homes. Water is precious, and makeup symbolizes wealth, leisure, and success. If a village woman is seen by others as overindulging in either of these two (or other) vanity items, she risks public censure. Samira further highlights the potential danger of the use of these items even when alone to risking punishment from the jinn.

Propriety is maintained through the public enactment of certain norms and rules of modesty and work. Yet even when alone for only a little while, a woman's actions are watched by the jinn. This feeling of being constantly watched and never being entirely alone is at times oppressive: a woman must constantly strive to behave in proper ways, or, less directly, in Samira's words, a woman may feel "there's always something to do." It may be that the jinn are the only witnesses to a woman's actions, but even their presence reminds women of the need to be careful to maintain proper morality, as you never know who may be watching. Jinn stories often address issues of loneliness and isolation among women who are heavily burdened by the demands of housekeeping and childrearing alone in their homes. The antisocial nature of certain kinds of housework, or of acts of self-indulgence when far from the sight of neighbors, suggests a metaphorically similar position of the jinn and one's neighbors, as well as the risks of being alone.

Women's Work

The nature of women's work in Artas has changed dramatically in the space of a generation.[5] In the 1920s Artas was primarily an agrarian village, and both women and men worked in the fields. Elderly women whom I interviewed bemoaned the loss of freedom entailed in agricultural work—freedom to walk to and from the fields, take produce to the market, or care for animals in their pastures. Today, women are more tightly bound to their homes and immediate neighborhoods than at any time in the recent past. One elderly woman told me:

> Before we could move freely, wherever and whenever we wished. But now . . . This is the only thing that is bad about today. We used to collect vegetables together, me, my daughters, my husband, my sons, everyone, and we put them in baskets and we sold them in Bethlehem. At the end of the day at night we all left the land and made dinner together, me, my husband, and my children. Because I was working on the land I was not able to bake the bread, so my neighbors often made the bread for me. Sometimes the neighbors worked with us in the fields, if there was too much work for us alone. But things are different now. Now everyone does their own work in their own house.

Young women's mothers lived in extended family households and received assistance from other family members in their daily work. This older generation feels that their work was in many ways harder than that of young women today. They lacked washing machines, running water, electric ovens, television sets, and other modern conveniences. Young women's grandmothers were likely to have worked in fields with their husbands at various points during the year. Nowadays there are no young women who work in agriculture and very few men who support their families through agriculture alone. The continuing shift to nuclear family households supported by wage labor means that younger women do their housework mostly by themselves, and in larger houses than those maintained by their mothers and grandmothers.

Households in Artas have become increasingly nuclear largely because of sons' roles as wage-earners, which enable them to build their own homes. Of the eighty-one families interviewed in Artas in 1975, 50 (62 percent) lived as independent nuclear families; of the remaining 31, 18 included three generations—parents, married sons, and their sons' children. Three families included the father's parents and four households were shared with married brothers (Antonosky, Meari, and Blanc 1975: 22). Today it is relatively rare for married sons to live with their parents after the first year or two of their marriage. Most sons soon have a separate house, although many live above or below their relatives, in apartment-style homes.

Women young and old speak constantly of their *shughl*, or daily work. This work is a constant source of conversation and complaints. *Shughl* includes work done both in and outside of the home, such as sweeping and mopping the floors, washing the dishes, doing the laundry, airing the sleeping mats, cooking lunch, taking care of the children, baking bread, and doing the shopping. *Shughl* is often used as evidence by women that their lives are hard. Countless times I heard the comment, "You see! You see how hard our *shughl* is." Women do not feel free to socialize until their *shughl* is finished, although some socializing while doing *shughl* is acceptable. Though women will often send one of their children to ask a neighbor or relative to come and help his or her mother with her work, such as filling grape or cabbage leaves for lunch, in general, most kinds of *shughl* are not shared.

The importance of doing her own *shughl* properly is key to a woman's sense of self-esteem and accomplishment, and is taken as proof of symbolic cleanliness and a good way of life. Thus village women will often spend long periods meticulously and repeatedly sweeping the area in front of their homes, for example—areas that may be tiled but usually end at an unpaved dirt road. While at first this seemed to me to be a tremendous waste of effort and time, I believe now that it is a public demonstration for women that their homes are "clean" in both the symbolic and literal sense and that they work hard to keep them so. A married woman who does not do her *shughl* properly (and make at least some of it visible to her neighbors) risks marring her reputation as a clean, or morally upright, woman. Indeed, keeping one's laundry lines regularly full of washed clothes and sleeping mats visibly placed in the sun are also important and commented on by women about their neighbors (i.e., how many times during the week the laundry appears, how long it is left on the lines after it has dried, how often sleeping mats are placed outside in the sun, etc.).

Samira's story draws attention to this work that married women do—childcare, cleaning, and beautifying tasks. She critiques this work by arguing that it prevents women from focusing on God and therefore makes them vulnerable to attack by the jinn. Samira argues that a man is able to lead a more pious lifestyle than a woman whose work never ends. A man can come and go from his house and has time to read the Qu'ran in the evening. Women do not have such free time—or freedom. Women are vulnerable to attack, lacking the opportunity to protect themselves through piety because of the demands of housework and childcare.

While women's work may necessarily keep them far from God and at risk from the jinn, men, who have far greater opportunity than women to be pious, learned, and morally upright, may in practice be similar in some respects to Samira's immoral jinn. Recall the jinn's acts of immorality: He is attracted to Samira at her most unclean and clean/beautiful moments, shows her mercy and then tries to choke her, disregards her status as a married woman, and has an arrogant and unpredictable character. He is, in short, the antithesis of a good village man. A man should not be attracted to a woman while she is menstruating or, indeed, to a woman wearing makeup who is not his wife; a man should not have an unpredictable temperament; a man should desire to marry an appropriate mate. This story of the jinn thus makes explicit implicit knowledge about male morality and men's fallibility in the realm of the jinn. We may extrapolate that Samira believes that human men also do not always act morally; indeed, men are capable of infidelity, unpredictable tempers, and immoral desires. In short, men may squander their greater opportunity to be morally upright.

Samira, the only woman I met in the village who smokes cigarettes (a luxury item firmly believed to be indulged in properly only by men), is known as a "strong" [*qawīyya*] woman, a description that contains a hint of reproach. She may indeed behave a bit too strongly at times to be considered demonstrating appropriate behavior. Through her story of the jinn, our attention is drawn to points of social critique of the requirements of morality for village women. Otherwise overlooked or minimized in daily practice and conversation, the requirements of village morality for women are revealed as, at times, oppressive and somewhat hypocritical. After all, these moral requirements—and the punishments for not adhering to these requirements—should, in theory, be as applicable to men as to women. Samira's jinn tells its listeners that in practice they are not.

* * *

While the jinn are known to exist because of the references in the Qu'ran to them, women's experiences with the jinn are locally elaborated, meaningful, and immediately relevant to their lives in the contexts of patriarchy, family roles, and gendered expectations. Women's jinn stories reflect on a range of criticisms and consequences they may have of this system and its structure. Here the context of Israeli occupation is not in the foreground, although it is never forgotten. In the following chapters we will turn to a detailed examination of a jinn story which looks at the intertwining and collusion of village forces and Israeli occupation for one young woman, as well as some men's experiences.

NOTES

1. The legal age for marriage in the West Bank is fifteen for women and sixteen for men. Hammami notes, however, "While these are the legal minimums, in practice the courts are much more flexible" (1994: 288). Hammami shows that for women in Nura's age group, 28 to 32 years of age, the median age for marriage was 18.4 (1994: 290).

2. Escribano argues that in the West Bank village in which she did her research the term *wisah* (a derivative of *wusikh*) was used most often to describe the refugees in the village, referring "not to their standard of cleanliness, but to their soiled honor" (1987: 167).

3. It is important to note that I am not claiming that this is always or necessarily true. My next door neighbor in Artas graduated first in her class from Bethlehem University and then married her first cousin. She insisted that they wait to marry until she finished her university education; he happily agreed. Yet this experience was a notable exception among the many young and middle-aged women I met; indeed, she was among the very few female university graduates I met while in Artas. Most people were deeply concerned about the effects of staying in school too long for a young woman chances for marriage, although the definition of "too long" varied somewhat from family to family.

4. Secondary schools for grades nine through twelve were opened for girls and boys in Artas in 2002; the first graduating class was in 2003. The schools take pupils from Artas and Deheisha refugee camp. I have been told by a number of villagers in our ongoing correspondence that the availability of a school within the village for girls that allows them to complete the necessary requirements for the *tawjihi* exams is strong encouragement for girls to stay in school until that point, if not beyond.

5. Crowfoot and Baldensperger (1932: 3-11) review the yearly agricultural cycle in Artas and its accompanying tasks before the shift to wage labor.

Chapter Four

Zahia and Her Jewish Jinn

One of the most complex and extended stories of the jinn that I recorded and followed while in Artas concerned a young woman I call Zahia. Her story draws together, critiques, and provides a range of insights into numerous moral practices and daily realities shaping life in Artas, including social geography, the Palestinian diaspora, the Israeli military and bureaucracy, Palestinian employment on Israeli construction sites, and the place of young women and their families in this complex world. I first learned about Zahia from my neighbors in the village who are close friends of her family (mentioned at the outset of chapter 1, as recorded in my field notes). I interviewed her brother as well as other family members and friends of Zahia, and later, when I traveled to Amman, Zahia herself. When I saw Zahia and spoke with her she stated that she was temporarily freed from the jinn.

A central piece of evidence for Zahia's past experiences of possession, in addition to the stories told by those who witnessed the events, was a cassette tape of one of Zahia's possession episodes when she was in the village. Her brother would often carry this tape around the village when visiting people and play it for them. I witnessed these tape-playing events numerous times during the course of my year in the village, eventually recorded one, and have included a translation of it below. Key to the claim that Zahia's jinn was Jewish is the fact that the jinn is recorded on tape as "speaking" in Hebrew; close listening to the tape reveals that the jinn used three Hebrew words. What is important here is that it was widely accepted and acknowledged by family, friends, and neighbors that the Jewish jinn "spoke" Hebrew through Zahia's mouth, even if the jinn "spoke" Hebrew, at best, symbolically.

From these various sources I learned that Zahia was sixteen when her family sent her for the first time from Artas to Amman in Jordan to marry her cousin, whom she had never met. It is relatively unusual for young women in the village to feel forced into marriage. Young women generally have some degree of influence in determining their future marriage partner. Zahia's situation, however, was different. Zahia's uncle's family had left the village to live in Amman before 1967 and found that they were unable to return to the West Bank after the Israeli occupation began. Thus Zahia joined a growing movement of young women between Artas and Amman, women who marry relatives so as to maintain family relationships strained by years of distance. Many young women will happily consent to such arrangements, but Zahia was not given a choice. Her father and uncle, in an attempt to affirm their family bonds, decided their children would marry and gave neither child a choice in the matter.

After the birth of her first child within a year of her marriage, Zahia was possessed by a Jewish jinn, as evidenced by the fact that she acted "possessed" (screamed, moved uncontrollably) and "spoke" (three words) in Hebrew. One night while under the spell of this Jewish jinn, Zahia tried to commit the most heinous crime imaginable for a woman—the murder of her infant son. After this thwarted attempt, her husband's family allowed her to return to Artas for treatment by the village sheikh. Zahia stayed with her natal family in the village for more than a year.

In the course of her treatment the sheikh asked the jinn who intermittently took active possession of Zahia while she was in the village what he wanted from her. The jinn answered that he wanted Zahia to be divorced by her husband. But, as Zahia's brother explained to me, "Our family refused to let her get divorced from her family." After many months of playing the Qu'ran on cassette next to Zahia's bed at all times, the village sheikh pronounced her cured and she returned to her husband's/cousin's family in Amman. Shortly afterwards, Zahia's condition again worsened. Again, she returned to the village for treatment, but this time the incidents of possession were worse. Zahia told me, "I needed six or seven men in order to stay sitting in a chair or to prevent me from doing bad things. They couldn't help me in Amman. So my brother came and got me and took me back to the village for treatment." The sheikh in the village determined not only that Zahia was still possessed, but that she was, in fact, possessed simultaneously by sixty-seven Jewish jinn. After six months with her family, Zahia was again pronounced cured due to the continuous reading of the Qu'ran in her presence, and she returned to Amman. My neighbor's news on the rooftop was a rumor that Zahia was once again having troubles in Amman.

The tape that Zahia's brother carried with him and played often was from one of Zahia's episodes of possession during a curing session with a sheikh. I include a translation of the transcript here.

Jinn: You want her to pray?

Sheikh: Yes. She just now prayed.

Jinn: You killed her.

Sheikh: But she has patience, God willing.

Jinn: You killed her. You are not with her [i.e., you don't help her].

Sheikh: But she has patience, right? Wait and you'll see what I am going to do to you.

Jinn: She's strong, strong.

Sheikh: She is strong from the strength of God. God supports her. God gives her strength.

Jinn: I am going to hurt her, to cause her pain.

Sheikh: God is going to hurt you, to cause you pain, because God gives her strength.

Jinn: Really, I am going to hurt her.

Sheikh: You can't do anything to her.

Jinn: Really, I am going to kill her, to kill her.

Sheikh: The guards which are here, do you see them? Don't you see them? [sheikh is referring here to his personal army of the jinn] Muhammed, our brother, he is a Muslim and he is the leader to the group [again referring to a specific jinn].

Jinn: *Lo, lo* [Hebrew, meaning no].

Sheikh: Do you see them?

Jinn: *Lo, lo*.

Sheikh: Now I want to bring them to kill you.

Jinn: *Lo, lo, lo*.

Sheikh: Really, our brother Muhammed God protects and supports, as well as Ahmad and Abdullah.

Jinn: *Lo, lo, lo*.

Sheikh: And Abd Al-Hadi.

Jinn: Liars! Liars!

Sheikh: Abd Al-Minam and Abd al-Rahman.

Jinn: Liars! Liars!

Sheikh: What do you mean liars? Now I am going to let them tear you into pieces. I am going to let them attack you! Speak! Why do you say no? Are you scared? Are you scared?

Jinn: Liars!

Sheikh: All of them are liars, really?

Jinn: Liars!

Sheikh: What are you?

Jinn: Just leave me alone! Just leave me alone!

Sheikh: Yes. I want to let them attack you.

Jinn: Just leave me! Just leave me!

Sheikh: [speaking to the jinn guard] Come and tear him into pieces, you Muhammed and your group, come to tear him into pieces.

Jinn: Leave me! Really, I am going to kill her.

Sheikh: Really—I am going to let them tear into pieces [voice rising], really tear you into pieces. The emperor that I converted [to Islam] and with him one million soldiers converted at the same time—in one night. Where is the emperor of the jinn now? In which country? Why don't you respond? Why are you escaping from these questions? One million converted to Islam! All of the army! Million in one night converted to Islam! What's happened, you rude one!? Why don't you respond? You stopped talking? You are afraid of the truth? You stopped talking, ya Yusuf [name of the jinn]? Speak to me, talk to me! Your aunt Kohana, do you know her? Kohana? The great queen of the jinn! Did you see her when she came with thunder and lightning? Kohana is not just anyone! Do you know what I did to her?

Jinn: You are a liar! You are a liar!

Sheikh: I put my feet in her stomach [i.e., I conquered her]. I cut her intestines into pieces [i.e., hurt her badly].

Jinn: You are a liar!

Sheikh: Everything for you is lies? You are the only one telling the truth?

Jinn: But I won't leave her, I won't leave her, don't press me [voice rising].

Sheikh: Who said to you that I am asking you to leave her? I am telling you that I am going to kill you inside of her!

Jinn: I won't leave her, I won't leave her!

Sheikh: I want to kill you inside of her.

Jinn: I won't die, I won't die.

Sheikh: I want to kill you inside of her.

Jinn: I won't die, I won't die, I love her, I love her [again, voice still rising].

Sheikh: I am the one who is going to kill you, I am going to kill you. Are you going to die by your own choice? Is there anyone who dies by choice? There is one who is going to kill you. Listen to the proverb I am going to tell you: the one who comes to you, knows how to deal with you. Really, I am going to hurt your liver! Are you scared, you coward?? Hey, you, coward! Are you scared? Hey you! You dog! You rude person! What did the Qu'ran do for you? What did it do for you? It is written on your forehead that you are an unbeliever! You are insulted! The unbelief is written on your forehead, you dirty one! Why don't you like Muslims? What did they do to you?

Jinn: *Lo*, Islam! [Hebrew, meaning no]

Sheikh: Why?

Jinn: Liars!

Sheikh: What proves to you that Muslims are liars? What did they do to you?

Jinn: I don't want them! I don't want them!

Sheikh: They decided to hang you!

Jinn: *Lo* Hamas, *lo* hamas, *lo* hamas! *Aravim* [Hebrew, meaning Arabs] are liars!!

Sheikh: We are going to hang you!

Jinn: There is nothing for you here! There is nothing for you here!

Sheikh: We are going to bring dynamite and blow your head off.

Jinn: *Lo, lo, lo.*

Sheikh: Bring me a stick in order to kill him.

Jinn: *Lo, lo*! You are a liar!

Sheikh: Bring me the stick! I am going to kill him! What's wrong with you? I will kill him by the strength of God. By the strength of God, dirty one! Don't you know that they named me the Victorious One by God! Hey, Kohana said to me, God named you the Victorious One by God because God always makes you victorious over us.

Jinn: *Lo*! My love! I won't leave her.

Sheikh: Who are you to say that you love her!?

Jinn: I won't leave her because of you! You are dogs!

Sheikh: You are the dog.

Jinn: My love, my love.

Sheikh: You control her enough to be able to call her 'my darling'?

Jinn: *Lo, lo, lo*! She's strong! I have to kill her! I have to kill her. *Lo*, Just wait until I leave her and then you will see what I am going to do.

Sheikh: The boy brought me a gun and I am going to kill you with it. My son brought me a gun! I am going to kill you!

Jinn: You'll see what I am going to do to you.

Sheikh: Do you see this gun? I am going to kill you with it, God willing! God insults you. You criminal. God insults you. Why did you hate Hamas?

Jinn: *Lo biseder, lo biseder, lo* Hamas [Hebrew, meaning, Not ok, not ok, no Hamas].

Sheikh: What did they do to you? What did they do to you?

Jinn: *Lo* hamas, *lo* hamas, *lo aravim* [Hebrew, meaning, No Hamas, no Hamas, no Arabs]

Sheikh: Did they kill your father?

Jinn: *Aravim*—all of them are liars.

Sheikh: What did they do to you?

Jinn: *Lo* hamas!

Sheikh: Now you have to choose—either I am going to kill you or you will convert to Islam!!

Jinn: *Lo* Islam, *lo* hamas, *lo* Islam, *lo* hamas!

Sheikh: You dirty one, I am going to kill you right now!!

Jinn: *Lo, lo, lo, lo, lo*! I hate Islam!

Sheikh: This is your last chance! Either you convert or I will let the guards attack you and tear you into pieces!

Jinn: *Lo* Islam.

Sheikh: Now you are going to die. Muhammed, Ahmad, Abd al-Rahman!!! Come! Fight! [voice rising]

Jinn: Leave me alone! [crying]

Sheikh: I am not going to let them leave you until you convert. Otherwise you will die.

Jinn: [in very pained voice while crying] Ok! Let him get away from me! I convert! I convert!

Sheikh: Are you sure? Are you sure? So you have to say, I witness that there is no God but Allah and Muhammed is his prophet.

Jinn: I witness that there is no God but Allah and Muhammed is his prophet! I convert!

Sheikh: Now that you are a Muslim you have to leave her and I will teach you about Islam.

Jinn: Ok, I leave her now.

When villagers listened to this tape, most focused on the fact of the jinn's use of Hebrew words. Villagers also noted the disjointed and strange nature of the dialogue, and interpreted it as evidence of Zahia's possessed state. The publicly shared ideas in Artas about village women's practices of morality, social relations, and their perceptions of Jews as explored in previous chapters are key background for understanding Zahia's case.

ZAHIA AND SOCIAL GEOGRAPHY

The timing of Zahia's first possession episode is significant—within the first year of her marriage and immediately following the birth of her first child—drawing our attention to these experiences as filled with a moral ambiguity that metaphorically opened the door for the jinn to attack. In this section I examine the circumstances and meanings of her marriage. The birth and symbolism of her son are examined in the following section.

Cousin Marriage

The stated purpose of Zahia's arranged, long-distance, cousin marriage was to maintain family ties among parts of the family that feel that their closeness (in both the literal and metaphorical sense) is threatened. Marriage between the cousins in such families is thus an attempt to bind together the family in the face of long-term and long-distance separation. When the children of siblings marry, villagers in Artas often express the sentiment that such marriages have the potential to turn out well. Few women expressed the sentiment to me that a marriage to a cousin is always better for a young girl, but they emphasized that it very possibly *could* be. This potential stems from two possible points: First, the parents of the bride and groom, as siblings, are likely to have each other's best interests at heart. Thus a girl's mother may feel that her daughter will be safe with her brother's or sister's son, the son of a sibling whom she knows intimately, emphasizing the nature of well developed kin relations. Second, if the cousins themselves have grown up together, almost as if they were siblings, then they are familiar with and care for one another. This aspect of the potential for a good relationship between the cousins emphasizes the role of proximity, or social geography. The sibling relationship, then, contains within it the possibility of fostering the closest kind of association, the kind informed by years of intimate familiarity and shared sentiment.

Indeed, siblings are intimately familiar with one another and will often have powerful emotional ties throughout their lives.[1] Suad Joseph describes the brother-sister relationship in Lebanon as one of "patriarchal connectivity inscribed as love" (1999: 116). Connectivity refers to the "psychodynamic processes by which one person comes to see himself or herself as part of another" (Joseph 1999: 121). This sense of connectivity can be seen in some practices in Artas. Brothers typically make a point of visiting their sisters, even those who may have married far from their natal family. Typically, a brother will bring his sister a gift on the occasion of the two holidays celebrated during the year (*'īd al-fiṭr and 'īd al-adḥā*). Sisters will also visit one another, lend one another money, and look after each other's children. The relations between siblings are, consequently, often characterized by generosity and a lack of a need for explanation or excuse.[2]

This perspective in many ways resembles Granqvist's insights into the nature of cousin marriage. To understand why cousins are believed to be the best possible mates for one another, Granqvist discussed, among other reasons, the roles of emotion and personal preference. For example, cousin marriages may be preferred by women in particular because they allow the bride to remain relatively close to her own immediate family. Granqvist quoted a poem told to her by an informant about the benefits of marrying one's cousin over a stranger:

> The cousin—my darling! How sweet it is on his breast to rest!
>   The stranger—the clumsy one! May he be wrapped in his grave clothes.
> (1931: 67)

Not only does cousin marriage allow a woman to remain near her own family, it may also ensure her better treatment. Granqvist described one possible rationale:

> A man need not have so much consideration for his wife if she is a stranger; he can give free rein to his anger and his curses. For in uttering a curse against someone a man, to increase its effect, curses the parents and ancestors and in this way the children, so that a man cannot curse his cousin-wife without at the same time cursing himself; if he curses her the curse goes back to the previous generation and then to the younger generations and finally to himself. This reason for self-control naturally does not exist when it is a stranger wife whom he curses whose root and origin are quite different. (1931: 94)

Lutfiyya, drawing from his work in Jordan, also argued that "it is believed that cousins would be more understanding as future mates than would total strangers" (1966: 130).

Of course, it is impossible to explain all cousin marriages in this way or any other. At times, a cousin marriage may be forced upon an unwilling couple; in other instances, young cousins may be in love. Yet recognizing the potential ties which may exist among siblings is an extension of the critical components of social geography—physical proximity, choice, and sentiment—in creating ties among villagers. Thus it is not enough to argue that siblings share a "blood" tie and are therefore close to one another. Rather, it is more accurate to say that siblings have the unique opportunity to be familiar with almost every aspect of each other's lives and, thus, the potential for becoming very close indeed. The marriage of their children may, at times, reflect these feelings of sibling closeness through "taking care" of the marriage of the other's child. Further, the expectation that cousins will fall in love and make good marriage partners informs young people's reactions to their cousins, contributing to their own sense of love and attraction to one another. Granqvist notes, "In countries where cousin marriage is highly esteemed it is likely that a man will have tender feelings towards his cousin" (1935: 60).

I highlight here the roles of familiarity and shared sentiment between siblings in their decision to arrange the marriages of their children; other theories of this practice have focused on the functions[3] or statistical occurrence[4] of cousin marriages. These theories obscure women's (and, indeed, men's) roles in the lives of their children. Women's capacity for caring is often lost by functionalists in the rush to find the "real" reason behind cousin marriages. Indeed, functionalist arguments both isolate and reify only one of many possible reasons at a particular time for certain kinds of marriages and leave an individual's (particularly a woman's) motivations and circumstances unexamined. Indeed, Bourdieu has pointed out that marriages such as FBD (a marriage between a man and his father's brothers' daughter), which may be identical genealogically for the anthropologist, may have "different, even opposite meanings and functions, depending on the strategies in which they are involved" for the families (1977: 48). Thus parallel cousin marriage may have contradictory meanings, since it is a product of a series of strategies, each of which may differ according to the interests of the individuals involved (Bourdieu 1977: 70).

Yet an emphasis on individual motivation and strategy suggests an assumption of maximizing gain and may be just as functionalist in this respect as earlier models. In contrast to these approaches, recognition of the roles of familiarity and shared sentiment for forming enduring ties leads to an acknowledgement of the special bond which may exist among siblings. This bond may be a more productive source of explanation for the arrangement of some cousin marriages than an emphasis on individual motivation or functionalism.[5]

Stranger Marriage

Zahia grew up in Artas where cousin marriages are arranged based on the experiences and expectations created by familiarity and shared sentiment. Her own marriage was intended to be one of these preferred, intimate marriages. Yet it was, in reality, more akin to a typical stranger marriage. While cousin and family marriages often correspond to a feeling of "closeness" among siblings or otherwise related family members, Granqvist called the brides of stranger marriages, "café brides." Such marriages were typically arranged by men who would go to sit in cafés to talk and smoke together and would often end up arranging the marriages of their children (1931: 99).[6] This general pattern is still common today. Men who work together or have come to know one another via mutual friends may arrange the marriages of their children for a number of reasons, among which the men's shared friendship is always one. Enemies and strangers do not arrange for their children to marry. Thus even for "café brides" some degree of shared sentiment may be a motivating factor in arranging a marriage in which the prospective bride and groom have never met. Such marriages create a legitimate context for bringing families closer in the future, both geographically and symbolically. As Granqvist comments, "Often one can see that a closer knitting of the bond of friendship between the parents is intended by the marriage of their children" (1931: 43).

On the other hand, women who have married into Artas as stranger brides will often try to arrange for a daughter from their own family or village also to marry into an Artasi family. Granqvist called this preference on the part of stranger wives "the marriage policy of the women" (1931: 96). In these cases, women are trying to maintain closeness to those they left behind in their own village. These women, Granqvist reports, will attempt to make a match for their children with a woman from either their natal family or village: "If they do not get a relative they will at least have someone from their own village" (1931: 96). This transforms affinal relations not only into kinship ones (cf. Boddy 1989) but also, importantly for the argument here, more closely located kinship relationships, as new brides move to their husbands' homes.

For Artasis who live in the Amman diaspora, the particular threats posed by stranger marriages are clear. One of Zahia's husband's close female relatives in Amman, Faiza, described to me how her two sons married "strangers": One married a Kuwaiti woman he met while studying in the United States. They now live in Kuwait. Her other son married an American while studying in the States and stayed there. Faiza's attitude toward these marriages is one of resignation. Faiza's sons' marriages demonstrate to Faiza (and others) that if a child goes far enough away, he/she can do as she pleases, and the desires of the family are no longer pertinent: proximity is central for enforcing familial ties and obligations. When proximity is replaced by distance, not only emotional ties but also relationships of power and authority are threatened. These latter relationships, like emotional ties, lose their force. She told me the following about her eldest son's return to the family in Kuwait (after finishing his studies in America):

> When he returned from America there were many ways he had been affected by the American community. The family and feeling of connection to us was limited for him. For example, if his brother is sick he wasn't affected that much. But when he came back and lived here for a while, he returned back to his nature. In the first few months when he returned from America, he would just go back and forth from his work to the house only. When he would come from work, he would just sit, watch TV, drink coffee, and did not ask if there were any problems in the house—he didn't care at all. After a while, his connection with the house and the family became strong again. His emotions and feelings towards his family and his country became stronger also.

Faiza understands her son's feelings of closeness to his natal family as dependent upon his ability to be near them and to refamiliarize himself with his family. Being in America for a number of years threatened that feeling of closeness, which had to be fostered in order to be regained, a comment which also demonstrates the socially constructed nature of kinship ties over their biogenetic origins.

Faiza's sister Lubna, also a long-time resident of the Palestinian diaspora (first in Kuwait and then in Amman) told me the following during our interview:

> *Do you prefer that your children will marry one from Artas or one from Amman or one from Kuwait?* I would love for them to marry one from Artas. Even now we are looking for a girl for Isma'in [in Amman], but I prefer to ask for a girl from Artas. Because I know all of them in Artas and they know me. Once when Isma'in was engaged to a girl from a village near Hebron who was living in Syria, her family was very difficult. The people in our village are very simple and kind, but the family from her village have very strong women who control their husbands. We got to know her in Syria; when we left Kuwait we went to Syria because we had a house there. We lived there about a year and a half. The girl was an orphan, I mean her father was dead. Isma'in's father when he came from Kuwait saw her. The girl was pretty and she studied only until the ninth grade. She entered Isma'in's father's mind and he spoke to Isma'in about her. Of course, Isma'in saw her because they would go and come to us. We engaged her for him and we wrote the marriage contract. I went to Syria because I wanted to see her and her family and they gave me the news. They said, we changed our minds. I asked them why and they said was that there was no reason, there just was no *nasīb* [fate]. Because of that I saw these people, and I dealt with them for a while, but I don't know what their psychology is or what is in their minds or their nature.

Why *ibn balad* [lit. son of my village]? I know who his mother and father are and their nature and how they behave and how they are living, while we don't know much about the stranger. I would also love for my girls to marry one from the village, it's better. One hopes that his daughter will be with one from his village, because he will be closer.

The future marriages of their children is a central issue for Lubna and Faiza, as it was for Zahia's uncle; all hope that their unmarried sons and daughters marry someone from Artas. This preference stems from their feelings of greater familiarity with the people of the village and, consequently, greater trust. Lubna's anecdote of Isma'in's broken engagement demonstrated for her the intrinsic unreliability of strangers. Villagers from Artas, however, are "closer," meaning here more familiar, knowable, and trustworthy. It further strengthens their identification as village members who are central to the give and take of village life, if not on a daily basis, then in certain key ways and moments.

Long distance marriages are not always easily arranged. Time apart has often changed family members' relations in spite of their best attempts to maintain them. Articulating the ways in which experiences of family are challenged by distance—notions that have been taken for granted by the older generation in particular—is difficult. Yet unsatisfying visits to Artas force the issue. Lubna told me the following:

> In the summer when we were there I was not happy honestly and my children did not enjoy their visit. We felt that there was a very big change. We felt that this time the people there changed more than the last time we were there. I mean, there was not that love, I thought they did not miss me like before, even my children are saying, that's it, we don't want to go there. We would love to return if there is any solution to the political problems there, but now my children are saying no way, we don't want to go there.

A woman from Jenin, a village in the north of the West Bank, witnessed the conversation I had with Lubna and eloquently added the following:

> [Leaving Artas] left a kind of hurt between the people outside and the people inside. Maybe the new generation does not have this hurt, so much, though. Maybe the cousins here in Jordan and the cousins in the West Bank will want to be together. But the older people are the ones who try to separate the young people. These older people say to their children, that the people who left wanted to go and live a much better life than those who stayed. . . . The new generation grows up without knowing us while the old generation doesn't accept our presence in their life.

The circumstances of occupation and the impossibility of those loved ones' return have strained the notion of family built on the practices of familiarity and reciprocity.

A 19-year-old woman from Artas who recently married her cousin in Amman told me:

> There are people there who don't care if we visit. The only people who are made happy by our visits are our close relatives—father, mother, brothers, and sisters. In the past, when one from outside the village came to visit, everyone appreciated it. But now, on my last visit there, I saw one of my distant relatives, and he didn't even say hi. I think this is because they are living under Israeli pressure.

Here the pressure of living under the Israelis is invoked as a way of understanding what otherwise seems to this young woman as a desertion of love following her recent departure from Artas. Her impression of the changed nature of her relationships to those she has left behind is based on her recent departure; one wonders how she will feel as time continues to pass.

Zahia's natal family and extended family in Amman clearly wished to strengthen their family ties through the marriage of their children. Yet Zahia's comment—that her cousin did not feel like a cousin at all—again directs our attention to geographical proximity as a central component of family identity. Being physically close to one another and engaging in daily acts of reciprocity and familiarity are central factors in creating the "kind of family that matters." Being a stranger wife in the village is generally pitied by villagers and believed to be far more difficult than if a woman stays near her own family. Zahia's marriage was arranged on the premise of more closely allying the families of two brothers, but this premise clashed with Zahia's own experiences and with the implicit definition of what family is: family cannot be people one has never known as neighbors and friends. Thus Zahia found herself in a paradoxical situation—she was marrying a cousin whom she could not think of as a cousin at all. Yet in the face of her father's and uncle's determination that the marriage go through, and the public praise that accompanies the announcement of a marriage of cousins (and the censure if such a marriage fails), Zahia had little choice.

That Zahia was possessed for the first time while in Amman points to her new physical place of residence as well as her symbolic social location as dangerous sites, arenas which enabled the jinn to attack. Zahia, as a young bride, married to a stranger and residing far from home, was alone, if only metaphorically, and thus vulnerable to attack. The jinn are drawn to symbolically and practically dirty and dangerous spaces, such as garbage dumps and Israeli prison cells (discussed in the following chapter), as well as locations far from the site of other people. Here, we must consider the presence and attack of the jinn in Amman, in Zahia's marital home, as suggestive of her moral evaluation of these locations.

ZAHIA'S JEWISH JINN

Reports of Jewish spirits are not unique to the West Bank. Crapanzano (1977b: 150) describes how in Morocco the demon husband of the demoness Lalla 'A'isha and Lalla 'A'isha herself spoke to a man in the "Jews' language." The Christian Amhara and Jewish Falasha in Ethiopia have *zar* spirits who are Christian, Muslim, Jewish, and pagan (Kahana 1985: 128). In Zahia's case, however, the Jewish jinn behaves in politically charged ways which reflect on a range of experiences with a specific group of human Jews.

What is known about the Jewish jinn that possessed Zahia? Two key pieces of evidence were pointed out to me repeatedly as demonstrating not only that Zahia's jinn was a Jewish jinn but also that it had (human) Jewish characteristics: first, that the jinn attempted to murder Zahia's son and, second, that the jinn spoke Hebrew. That Zahia's Jewish jinn tried to make Zahia murder her infant son is analogous to (and made understandable by) the fact that human Jews murder or, less directly, co-opt, the sons of Palestinian women. Zahia's Jewish jinn, by seeking the murder of her infant son, may be understood as acting out the danger posed to young men by Israel and the relative powerlessness of the mothers of those young men to safeguard their sons. This action by a dangerous "Other" belonging to the realm of jinn thus also reflects on the complex and different ways in which many young Palestinian men and women experience contact with Israel.

In contrast to Zahia's ignorance and inexperience in matters involving Israel, her father's and brothers' nonchalance and familiarity in dealing with the Israeli bureaucracy and military were striking. By moving outside of the West Bank, Zahia became embroiled in the bureaucracies of both Israel and Jordan. Not only was she going far away, but she would have to deal with the uncertain process of waiting for a visa for her return to the village or a relative's visit to her in Amman. Israeli control over the visa-granting process for Zahia's return to the village is threatening and foreign; marginally literate and inexperienced in filling out forms and waiting in offices, Zahia entered into a world about which she admittedly knew nothing and in which she felt powerless.

In contrast to Zahia's inexperience with movement across borders and interactions with Israelis, Zahia's brothers and father, like many Artasi men, worked inside Israel on Israeli construction sites. Zahia's father and brothers work building Israeli homes, and sent her to Amman. Many women (and, of course, men) believe that contact with Israelis, if not always physically dangerous, is always potentially morally problematic (discussed further in the following chapter). Women find themselves far from the sites of their husbands' and brothers' places of work, and far from being able to create a change in the situation. Often women in the village must justify to themselves and at times to others, why their husbands and sons work building Israeli settlements both in the West Bank and in Israel.

Recognizing that such labor works against their own interests by extending and objectifying Israeli control over Palestinian space, yet equally cognizant of the fact the chances of finding other sources of work are slim, women (and, indeed, men) find themselves facing a troubling moral dilemma. The control of land is control of social geography: Palestinian men who work building Israeli settlements are thus extending Israeli control over and infiltration into their lives. Zahia's brothers and father contribute, therefore, not only to their own oppression but also to that of Zahia and other women in the village. Ironically, Israelis both create boundaries (between villagers and their relatives in Amman, for example) and enforce proximity (as in the case of Palestinian and Israeli male construction workers). Zahia dramatically experiences this irony; her Jewish jinn implicitly tells us so.

Thus Zahia's experience points to yet another highly problematic situation. The means by which her family supports and maintains itself (and therefore has the means by which to arrange her marriage) stems from the very forces that led to her uncle's family's inability to return to the village, and that may threaten her own possibilities for returning and visiting her family on a regular basis. For Zahia, the Jews and her relatives are in an uncomfortable, dangerous, and immoral pairing in much the same idiomatic vein as Zahia's Jewish jinn has immorally worn her.

Speaking Hebrew

Zahia also "spoke" in Hebrew when possessed by the Jewish jinn. Speaking Hebrew is a highly symbolic act, as well as a practical one, for Palestinian men and women. Time and again during my initial few visits to homes in Artas in which the husband worked in Israel or on Israeli settlements, I was forced to listen to a lengthy recitation of all the Hebrew words the man knew (including words typically associated with construction such as wall, ceiling, floor, cement, and words which reflected more general knowledge, including various phrases of greeting, the terms for relatives, etc.). Such recitations would sometimes consume my entire visit of an hour or two to the home. The man's wife, in the meantime, would invariably sit in the room, silent and with what seemed to me to be a disapproving look on her face, or continue her cleaning activities; in either case, she did not participate in the "conversation." Only after I had visited these homes a few times was I able to escape my Hebrew vocabulary lesson and speak with the women of the household.

In contrast to such men, the majority of Israeli and Palestinian young women do not share workplaces, familiarity, or language. As discussed, Palestinian women often feel that Israelis pose a moral threat to Palestinian ways of life. Palestinian women thus often express the need to uphold the divide between themselves and Israelis by expressly rejecting Israeli ways (such as Israeli women's excessive *ḥurrīya*). A key component of this rejection is also seen in village women's refusal to speak or learn Hebrew, a potent symbol of Israelis and their foreign ways. While this refusal may be viewed as circumstantial—village women do not work for long hours with Israelis and therefore do not need to learn Hebrew—Artasi women understand their lack of knowledge of Hebrew as *resistance*. They make no effort to learn Hebrew words from their male kin and openly criticize Israelis on moral grounds.

While women disapprove of their male kin's absorption of this foreign language and exposure to Israeli culture, some men demonstrate their knowledge of Hebrew with pride as proof that they have learned how to get along in and financially benefit from the world of their occupiers. Of all the universities in the West Bank, only Bethlehem University offers Hebrew language courses (taught at the time of my fieldwork by an Arab Israeli who also taught Arabic to Israelis). My research assistant studied Hebrew for two years at the university, arguing that knowing Hebrew might help him "get ahead" when he graduated; he further noted that his class was overwhelmingly male. Young people in other parts of the West Bank learn Hebrew only by exposure. Such gendered differences in men's and women's exposure to and evaluation of Hebrew and its symbolic importance are rarely stated directly, although these differences become more explicit in stories of the jinn.

What emerges from examining Zahia's story is that, in short, to speak Hebrew a woman must be possessed. As I mentioned, from the recording of one of her episodes of possession by the jinn it is clear that Zahia used three Hebrew words: the Hebrew word for "no" (lo, as opposed to lā in Arabic), "ok" (*biseder*), and "Arabs" (*Aravim*)—three of the most widely known Hebrew words in the West Bank. These words also carry symbolism beyond their common meanings: the ability to say "no" in the occupiers' language, for example, is surely significant. Knowing the name your occupier uses to describe you, *Aravim*, suggests an insider's knowledge about Arabs and their names. *Biseder* further suggests an intimate insider's knowledge of a commonly used phrase to mean ok, good, or fine—one that suggests an easy familiarity with speaking Hebrew. These words were evidence enough for her friends, relatives, and neighbors to repeatedly tell the story of how Zahia's Jewish jinn "spoke" Hebrew through her.

Although Zahia's father and brothers regularly demonstrate their competence in Hebrew, Zahia's Jewish jinn, by speaking even a few Hebrew words through her, emphasizes for those who listen that the acquisition of Hebrew should not be considered a form of symbolic capital but rather evidence of a problematic state or a moral transgression. Zahia's Jewish jinn indicates that those who have become even moderately fluent in Hebrew should not be lulled into a false sense of complacency. The moral threat to Arabic-speaking Muslims posed by contact with Jews cannot be overestimated. As Akin argues for stories of alien spirits in Kwaio in the Solomon Islands, these stories may "frame and conceptualize the process of cultural borrowing. In this scenario, individuals are seduced or pressured into careless cultural borrowing and thereby undermine ancestral culture and Kwaio society" (1996: 149). The Jewish jinn in this story is a warning to those who listen that the easy adoption of Hebrew may threaten Palestinian self- and nationhood.

Further, by speaking Hebrew, Zahia's Jewish jinn draws our attention to the fact that most Palestinian women feel that they reject learning and speaking Hebrew. Importantly, Zahia does so only when possessed, signaling the moral transgression of the jinn into her body. Men may speak Hebrew at any time, but in contrast, women do so only under conditions of extreme duress. Thus the warning implied in the acts of Zahia's Jewish jinn is addressed most specifically to Palestinian men. Zahia herself is relatively powerless to warn her male relatives of the moral encroachment of Israeli ways. But the rarity of a village woman speaking Hebrew, an act which can be understood only as a consequence of her possession, draws attention to the fact that Palestinian women should not under normal conditions speak Hebrew and, by extension, neither should Palestinian men.

Women's Bodies

Zahia's story of possession may be seen as an expression of her feelings not only about marrying an unknown cousin—almost a contradiction in terms—in a faraway place, but also about being subjected to the whims of an oppressive foreign bureaucracy and military that financially supports her family. Her story of spirit possession reflects on both the collusion of patriarchal and political hegemony and her own attempts to understand these oppressive and morally problematic situations. Thus Zahia's story may form part of an implicit discourse on power in which women comment on the dictates and paradoxes of both village life and the Israeli military through the idiom of possession by a Jewish jinn. As Boddy argues for the Sudan, "As it is in women's bodies that the mores of Hofriyati culture are inscribed, so to women's bodies we must look for villagers' statements on how the external world impinges on their own" (1989: 269).

Palestinian women such as Zahia may represent a particular point of vulnerability, a point that comes under attack by the Jews via the jinn. A 25-year-old woman in Bethlehem told me the following about the relationship between the jinn, the Jews, and Palestinian women:

I spoke to a sheikh about the jinn and he told me that because of the problems between us and the Israelis, the Jewish jinn try to prove their strength in our world, especially with respect to the Palestinians. The sheikh said that because of the problems between the Jews and the Arabs the jinn try to play their part in these problems and participate. So the Jewish jinn have begun to wear the Muslim women. The jinn try to prevent the women they are wearing from praying, or from reading the Qu'ran.

Who asks the jinn to play this role?

The jinn saw the problems and they decided by themselves to play this role. They try to bother the Arabs and especially the Palestinians by wearing the women because the women are the most valuable thing for the Arabs— especially a woman, like, a woman who is studying at the university. Only the women, seldom, seldom do the jinn wear a man. The sheikh told me that the number of women wearing the jinn is rising.

An invasion by jinn of women's bodies is an invasion of the most intimate realm that bypasses the streets where the first intifada took place. No longer solely a matter of publicly visible acts of oppression (such as shooting rubber bullets, or throwing canisters of tear gas), Israeli domination also includes more subtle acts. The usurpation of women's bodies through possession by spirits—understood at least in part by some villagers as a carefully orchestrated move by Israelis who have influence in the realms of the jinn—is a matter of moral pollution as well as a physical force. A woman who "wears" a Jewish jinn is thus a public reminder of Israeli infiltration, an infiltration of the most intimate kind.

THE JEWISH GIRL AND THE JINN

One story I heard turns the tables of a discussion of Jewish jinn and Palestinian women to Jewish women and Palestinian treatment of the jinn. This story reflects on aspects of Zahia's story discussed here from a different perspective. It is interesting to note that Jews also have experiences with spirits— experiences that closely resemble those of the Palestinians with the jinn. During the time I spent in the West Bank, a weekly Hebrew newspaper ran a lengthy story in its weekend supplement on Jews affected by the *dybbuk*, or, spirit of a dead person (Negev 1995). Similarities between the dybbuk and jinn include bodily possession of a human being (including speaking and acting through the human host), treatment through the reading of prayers near the afflicted person's ear, and the exit of the spirit through the little toe of the left foot so as to leave as small a scar as possible.

Often, village women's sense of their moral superiority to Jewish Israelis is reflected in certain stories of the jinn in which Israeli women are possessed and can only be cured by Muslim sheikhs. Sheikhs often told me that they had treated many Jews as well as Christians. Villagers, too, were convinced that the Jews must deal with unwelcome spirits. One young Artasi woman told me:

Once there was a daughter of a Jewish man. When she was taking a bath the jinn hit her. She was the man's only daughter. He took her to doctors in many countries, outside of Palestine, but they could not do anything for her. One of her hands could not move and one of her eyes could not blink. So they took her to a sheikha in Tekoa. The doctors at Hadassah [an Israeli hospital in Jerusalem] were making fun of her father for taking her to an Arabic doctor. They said, "You took her to many doctors in many countries and they couldn't help. You must be mad to think this woman can do anything!" The sheikha asked the man if he could stay with his daughter for seven days [for the course of the treatment]. The sheikha began to treat the daughter and after the seven days she recovered. On the seventh day all the doctors from Hadassah came to see that she was recovered and they could not believe their eyes. Out of happiness, the girl's mother had a heart attack, but she recovered. The girl's father tried to give the sheikha a lot of money but she would not accept it. She said, "If you really want to help me, what I want is permission from the Israeli authorities to build a house."

Only the sheikha has the ability to cure the Jewish girl, while only the Jews have the power to grant the sheikha the permission to build the house she wants. The former power relation speaks to Israel's inability to completely dominate the Palestinians and their failure to be more powerful at all things than the villagers, particularly in the realms of morality and religion. Yet the latter power play—that between the sheikha and the Israeli permission-granting procedure—is also central here. The sheikha's request for permission is a heartbreaking reminder of the entrenched nature of Israeli power in the West Bank. Israeli power may be challenged and, indeed, may in fact be found wanting in terms of morality and religion, but Israeli power over key aspects of Palestinian life is both obvious and deeply penetrating.

Here we see how the assumption of the greater moral power of Islam—the sheikha has the ability to cure the girl, not her Israeli doctors— quickly turns into a discussion of repression, including the insidious ways Palestinians are drawn into the hegemony of Israeli bureaucratic and economic ideas and practices. The sheikha must (indeed, is forced by the circumstances of the occupation) ask the Israelis for the permit she desires to build her house. This paradox is reminiscent of the bind in which Zahia's male relatives find themselves: Anxious to marry Zahia to a close male relative in a moral bid to strengthen family ties, to do so they are increasingly beholden to and dependent upon work for the Israelis for the financial means to make the marriage possible, and simultaneously prevented by the Israeli bureaucracy and military from regularly and easily being close. Power circulates here from moral high ground to problematic acquiescence (no matter how unwilling)—asking for bureaucratic favors in the case of the Jewish girl, and relying on work on Israeli settlements in the case Zahia's family—and back again. Indeed, the issues at stake are so interrelated that we are forced to contemplate whether a moral high ground can be maintained when it is used to "buy into" Israeli bureaucratic procedures or construction work, or, conversely, if the practices of Israelis are not powerful enough to address even their own needs.

* * *

Zahia's story of possession eloquently weaves together the strands of social geography, jinn possession, Israeli control, and village patriarchy, commenting on the powerful and oppressive demands of each force. The fact that Zahia's jinn was Jewish reminds us of Lambek's (1996: 243) observation that "spirits are intrinsically connected to the contexts in which they appear." Young people's knowledge of spirits stems from a local context in which religious identity is in the foreground and deeply politicized. It is thus significant that Zahia's jinn is not a Christian, Muslim, or unbeliever, but a Jew. Zahia's Jewish jinn— by invading her body, taking over her actions, speaking through her mouth, and attempting to murder her infant son—may be performing gendered bodily analogues to Zahia's new experiences of control by Israel. The Jewish jinn came to her following her move to Amman, her marriage, and the birth of her first child, a period in which her relationship to Israel became far more direct and problematic, even when compared to her sightings and experiences of harassment from Israeli soldiers in the village during the intifada. Throughout the intifada Zahia was subject to roughly similar degrees of harassment from the Israelis as other village women; now, however, Zahia has been singled out to interact with Israel on a new level. The Jewish jinn demands Zahia's body to move and speak in certain ways; it is unpredictable, forcible, and mean.

Yet the experience of Israeli power is only one aspect of Zahia's experience. We know that Zahia also felt pressured into an unwanted marriage, is far from home, and will not be allowed to divorce. The forces of patriarchy in the village and Israeli domination come together and strengthen one another, from Zahia's perspective. Indeed, her story invites comparisons with a Jewish jinn (which caused the body of a young village woman to speak Hebrew and act violently), human Jews, village women who are not possessed, and village men. The significance of Zahia's story thus goes beyond the illumination of Zahia's personal circumstances, no matter how important those details may be.

Zahia's story of possession also contributes to our understanding of the role of the jinn in policing moral boundaries. Jinn insist on the enactment of proper behavior even when women (and men) may be alone and out of sight of neighbors and friends, as discussed in the previous chapters. Emerging from these discussions was the idea that men and women are never entirely alone; even when they have no human companion, the jinn are omnipresent. The boundaries of moral behavior in these cases are extended to include all of an individual's actions. The sense of "private" as opposed to "public" space is thus redefined. In Zahia's case the jinn directs our attention to proper behavior for Palestinian men when they are far from the eyes of their neighbors and family. Instead of being alone, however, men in these cases are with Israelis. Propriety is threatened here, but not solely from a failure to recite the proper blessings before baking bread, or other overt acts. Palestinian men's potential exposure to (or even adoption of) Israeli immorality may not seem, on the surface, to affect men's lives in the village. They may appear to be unaffected by this contact. Yet Zahia's Jewish jinn suggests that the impropriety of village men, even when unseen or far from village women, may affect both men and women. The actions of Zahia's brothers and father establish the necessary context for her possession by a Jewish jinn.

Finally, it is interesting to recall that Zahia's original single Jewish jinn multiplied into 67 Jewish jinn as time passed and her situation did not change. The message may be that even temporary complicity with the Jews will only create more problems later. Of course, there may also be some significance to the correlation between the fact of Zahia's 67 Jewish jinn and the year 1967, when Israel's occupation of the West Bank began (but only Zahia and her Jewish jinn know about that).

By providing a means of articulating her experiences, Zahia's story of possession may reflect most powerfully not on her ability to resist her situation but, as Abu-Lughod (1990: 332) argues, on the "range of specific strategies and structures of power" to which she is subject. This range includes moral as well as physical domination by Israel, as well as the oppressive forces at work in village life. That Zahia is continuously reinserted into the same situation (her marriage in Amman) after her treatment speaks to the durability of these powerful forces. While her experience of possession may allow her room to negotiate how often and for how long she is able to return home, she is nonetheless only temporarily altering her situation. Spirit possession in this cultural context is allowed for as a temporary expression, but treated through a cure. Eventually a sheikh rids the person of the jinn and life returns to "normal," or the person will be dealt with as someone who is not wholly mentally competent.

NOTES

1. Boddy notes a similar closeness between siblings in Hofriyat, Sudan: "the bond between a brother and sister is exceedingly strong in Hofriyat and remains so despite their respective marriages" (1989: 82).

2. Sororate and levirate marriages (and their variations, such as giving a relative of the wife who died to the widower, if not the dead woman's sister) are reportedly practiced in Artas, although I did not hear of any cases. Granqvist noted that sororate and levirate marriages were explained by villagers who said that the death could not separate the relationship established by marriage between the families (1931: 86).

3. Functionalist arguments, stemming primarily from the work of anthropologists in other parts of the Middle East but echoed by some researchers in the West Bank, offered explanations that can be divided into three types: first, father's brother's daughter (FBD) marriage was believed to be a means of preserving property in the family (for example Antoun 1972: 140, 141; Granqvist 1931: 78; Rosenfeld 1968: 747–48). This line of argument depends on the Islamic rule of inheritance being upheld; the ethnographic record for many cases in the Middle East indicates that these rules are often ignored (Granqvist 1935: 256; Khuri 1970: 600; Murphy and Kasdan 1959: 17; Rosenfeld 1960: 66). Second, FBD marriage was viewed as a way for a man to increase his influence or that of his lineage in the community (for example Antoun 1972: 141; Barth 1954: 171; Rosenfeld 1968: 747-48). This rule-based account of behavior and loyalty at times coincides with villagers' practices and always coincides with a male, formalized discourse on the nature of relations, but does not do justice to the complexities of villagers' relations to one another. Third, and most peripheral to the case of Artas, FBD marriage was understood as a "custom that reflects and strengthens the segmentary character of the unilineal system of descent among Arabs" (Khuri 1970: 598).

4. In addition to various functionalist approaches, statistical approaches to understanding FBD marriage have focused on its frequency rather than the "content of [its] social value" (Khuri 1970: 598). See Ayoub for the argument that its occurrence is statistically unremarkable (1959: 274); her findings correlate with those of Barth (1954) and Granqvist (1931). Indeed, Gilbert and Hammel's (1966) computer simulated model demonstrated that FBD marriage may not be statistically significant when analyzed with respect to the preference for territorial endogamy.

5. My use of the term "shared sentiment" differs from Abu-Lughod's notion of sentiment as part of a "discourse of honor" in which only particular publicly sanctioned sentiments are appropriate (1986: 205). I use the term to refer to women's individual preferences for attachment to others on an intimate level, while recognizing that those preferences are restricted and structured by village social mores.

6. Granqvist further notes that the occasion of artisans' or guests' visits to the village, or women's trips to the market, may also precipitate arranged marriages, as these opportunities gave men and women the chance to see one another (1931: 101–4).

Chapter Five

Men and the Jinn

Hebron, April 5, 1996

Abu Zuhair (AZ): Why are you interested in the jinn?

Celia: Well, I've never read about the jinn in Palestine. So when I heard stories about them I was fascinated.

AZ: You have to ask yourself why the jinn are here. You have to realize what is going on here. I am an educated man, educated in politics, society. I have read a lot. You are not speaking with just anybody here! And I am telling you that the Israelis use the jinn to affect those who are vulnerable. Especially those who are arrested and put in their prisons. You can research this point. You will find that nearly 10 percent of the men who have been in Israeli prisons have had problems from the jinn. You have to ask about this.

I've read the Israeli Talmud, if you know what that is. It is not their holy book itself, it is something separate from the Holy Book. It is how to deal with people, the Jews themselves. They use the jinn to punish us.

Zuhair (son of Abu Zuhair): Did you choose this subject by yourself or did someone send you? [Turns to his father:] Because it is different than if someone sent her or if she has a problem herself and she wants to reach a solution.

[My research assistant steps in to explain how I came to the West Bank from a Canadian university to better understand the Palestinians and became interested in stories of the jinn.]

[long pause]

AZ: The Israeli rabbis know about the jinn. I sat with one of them two years ago. We were talking about the situation, about their land, as they call it, and then I put the word jinn in our discussion. He became very nervous and said, "Israel

99

is a Holy Land. There are no jinn here. In all the rest of the world there is jinn, but there are none in Israel." I tried to ask him some more questions. I found, at last, that they knew about the jinn exactly. They have Jewish jinn. They use the jinn to punish the Palestinians, the Christian and the Muslim Palestinians. They use the jinn to punish us just like the Jewish people are punishing us. You must believe me. There is a lot of evidence for this, particularly in the prisons. I mean, there are men who go into prisons good and kind people and come out completely changed. They are like crazy people when they leave the prison, but when they went in they were fine. They do strange, unnatural things. And these jinn who affect these men are certainly controlled by the Jewish rabbis. They control them in order to punish us, to make troubles for us. But in Israel, they say, there are no jinn! But all the jinn in Palestine are Jewish! Most of the jinn in Palestine are Jewish jinn.

Zuhair: Not all of them.

AZ: I know not all of them, but most of them. I think you can tell that all the cases that the sheikh here has treated, the jinn who were wearing these cases were Jewish jinn. Why? Think about this! All the jinn that make troubles for us are Jewish! Ask yourself, why are these jinn not Christian? Why is he not an unbeliever? Why is he not a Muslim? Why is he only Jewish?! . . . These problems will not decrease, either. They will only increase! This is because there is no peace here! Do you see the murder that still goes on? Do you see everything that they are still doing to us? This is no peace. This is nothing like peace. So the jinn will only continue, probably doing more to punish us than ever before. You must know this. Write it in your book.

Zahia's case suggests the ways in which Israeli occupation and its effects may be experienced by women in the intimate realms of their homes and marriages. Stories of men who have had encounters with the jinn in Israeli prisons share this emphasis on the less publicly visible experiences of Israeli domination. These jinn stories thus complement studies that have analyzed how prisons may function as "academies" of nationalism and resistance education for Palestinian men (Ya'ari 1989); how bodily violence endured by young Palestinian men in the occupied territories is related to the construction of masculinity (Peteet 1994); and the roles of women in creating young men as moral persons (Jean-Klein 2000). As Abu Zuhair argues, many stories link Palestinian men's experiences with the jinn and Israeli prisons, and the variation in these stories is marked. I discuss just four episodes, including one story featured in a popular magazine, in this chapter.

These stories share not only a sense of the physical hardships of prison life but also the concept of prison itself as a place of moral pollution, a place in which men become demoralized and feel threatened. Congruent with the logic of social geography, prisoners, not surprisingly, experience their physical dislocation as socially and emotionally disruptive. If the jinn are particularly likely to disturb women when they are alone, as a kind of omnipresent neighbor—they are also drawn to men who suffer enforced loneliness while imprisoned. In addition, in popular belief, the jinn are often associated with places that may be either literally or symbolically dirty, such as garbage sites or bathrooms. Here prison is aligned with those places of dirt, and the prisoners, therefore, are subject to the defilement that accompanies it. The elements of social dislocation, isolation, dirtiness, and the presence of the jinn are a powerful combination of social, physical, and spiritual forces for men in prison.

HAMID

The first of these stories was told to me by a young man in Artas named Hamid. Hamid spent an evening telling me, the family with whom I was living, and a number of our neighbors about his time in an Israeli prison during the intifada. In a calm voice and with an occasional touch of black humor, he talked about his weeks of solitary confinement, days of being forced to stand in a room smaller than a phone booth, and the total lack of sanitary facilities. At the end of the evening, he told us how, at a time of severe depression and homesickness, a jinn came to him. Hamid could not see this jinn, but he felt its presence and heard its voice when the jinn told him his family's news. He heard of his sister's marriage, his brother's new baby boy, and how his parents longed for his release. Hamid was able to confirm that the jinn's information was correct when he was finally released.

Hamid's story is the least elaborated of the three I present here but it eloquently sets the tone for many stories in this strand of jinn stories. The arrival of the jinn—a jinn who is not evil—is correlated with Hamid's most emotionally desperate time in prison. Removed from his "natural" place in village life, locked away, and unable to change his situation, Hamid may have found this jinn's visit empowering and comforting, however briefly. Indeed, the jinn here can be likened to a surrogate close relation, enabling him to reconstitute domestic space, at least imaginatively, within prison walls. For a moment, he knew what was happening to those he loved and was reminded that he does have a place in society and that it awaits him. That his place in the village is tied centrally to staying abreast of the news of his family and the neighbors who live there is articulated through the jinn who told him his family's news. Hamid did not want his knowledge of those he loved to lapse, a lapse which would have threatened his feelings of closeness to them and their feelings for him.

IBRAHIM

The second story is more elaborate than Hamid's. It was told to me by a 27-year-old Palestinian man, called Ibrahim here, who spent five years in an Israeli prison. He is now doing odd jobs in the Bethlehem area. I include part of our interview here:

> **Celia:** *When did the jinn come to you for the first time?*
>
> **Ibrahim:** I was in jail.
>
> **Celia:** *How old were you?*
>
> **Ibrahim:** I was 21 years old; now I'm 27.
>
> **Celia:** *Can you describe the first time the jinn came to you?*

Ibrahim: I was in a room in the jail. There was a person who lived in this room before me who suffered from problems with the jinn. The jinn wore him for nine years. At the beginning he suffered a lot because the jinn controlled him; that jinn was from the bad kind of jinn, he was like satan. The jinn affected him psychologically, it made him hysterical and he behaved like a crazy person. He abused other people—and all of these things were because of the jinn. He was worn by more than one jinn. The jail administration knew about his problems but they were unable to help because they can't do anything about jinn problems. So they brought a special person, an Arabic sheikh who was a prisoner also. His name was *Salah Shehada*. This sheikh stayed with the man for three months until he solved his problem by burning the jinn by putting fire on that person's body.

Then I came to that room, and some of the jinn were still there. The first months I felt something, but I didn't know that the jinn was inside me and others were watching me. It wasn't there all the time but at different moments. Sometimes I behaved strangely, unconscious of what I was doing. I used to forget what I would do. The first thing I felt were nightmares while I slept. I felt strange bodies shaking me and talking to me, so I used to wake up frightened. There came a time when I saw the jinn clearly, especially when I was alone or in the bathroom or at night, but most often when I was in the bathroom. It was a Jewish girl. She threatened to kill me. When she entered my body I felt tired, I wasn't able to do anything. I didn't want the people around me to know. But sometimes I would wake them up while they slept because I was talking in my sleep. After several months they thought that I had mental problems. This jinnia asked me to marry her for nearly seven months.

I was in prison for five years. When I knew that it was a jinn [causing these problems], I consulted one of the religious men who was there [in prison]. One of them was able to talk to her, and found out her name. The jinn have names, religions, and kings. Each one has a king. The king's name for her was Maimon Abnouf. The religious man asked the help of God and her king to let her enter my body and use my tongue. She spoke formal Arabic through me, and at the beginning her accent was like a Moroccan accent.

Celia: *Did you agree when she asked to marry you?*

Ibrahim: No. I didn't agree, because it is strange for a human to marry a jinn. I saw her once when she was putting on a mask. Her face was the ugliest thing I ever saw. The most beautiful one there [in the jinn world] is like the most ugly thing here. Her hair was white and stiff; her eyes were vertical, not horizontal like ours, her ears were big, she had fangs, long nails. The sheikh advised me not to agree to the marriage, too. Because if we married she would control me completely, everything about me. It is known that being mad is from the jinn.

She bothered me for thirteen months, but eventually the sheikh was able to make her leave me by asking the king from her kingdom to help me and with God's help. She didn't leave me the first time, but she took two weeks to leave from my body. So the jinnia left me though the big toe, because when the jinn leaves the body it scars the body in that place. She wanted to leave through my eyes, but eventually she left through my toes. So after she left she wanted to be friends, my sister. The sheikh did not want me to marry her, because of her religion, but after we were able to control her we told her that it was possible for her to be my sister under the condition that she agreed not to hurt me. When the jinnia left me, the sheikh woke me up and told me that I agreed and she agreed to be brother and sister. The jinn keep their promise, especially if they promise in front of the kings.

When the Israeli administration of the jail learned about me, they were afraid. I was in a military jail, in a security section. The prison is closed, so the guards are like the prisoners. When I was near a window or left my cell, the soldiers were afraid of me and would stay away from me. Sometimes they asked about the jinnia and when I would answer them they would become afraid. One of them had hysteria from the jinn, he thought that a jinn was wearing him. Every day or two I would call the jinnia. It was a way to entertain the other prisoners by talking to her. Some asked about themselves, their personal affairs, or would just want to talk.

Just as the jinn can haunt garbage dumps or bathrooms, so the jinn lingered in the prison cell in which Ibrahim found himself. This jinnia was Jewish, ugly, and desired Ibrahim to be her husband.[1] Once persuaded by a sheikh in the prison with Ibrahim, however, the jinnia became his friend, a metaphorical sister. The Israeli prison guards were afraid of Ibrahim because of his connection with the demon, while the other prisoners were entertained by Ibrahim and his jinnia.

Certainly one of the most vivid points of Ibrahim's story is that of power, specifically the reversal of power relations entailed by the Jewish jinnia: Ibrahim's Israeli guards were afraid of him, a clear reversal of the usual power relationship at work in the prison. Indeed, Ibrahim notes "the guards were like prisoners" in part because of the security of the prison which partially imprisoned them as well the prisoners, and in part because they feared Ibrahim's jinnia. It is also interesting to note that Ibrahim tells us that a guard thought that

he, too, was affected by a jinn and other guards were afraid; in contrast, the
other prisoners found both amusement and comfort in Ibrahim's jinnia. Like
the Jewish girl afflicted by the jinn discussed in the previous chapter, these
Jewish guards are not spared this spiritually-based problem. While only the
sheikha had the ability to cure the Jewish girl, here Ibrahim alone had the ability to control the Jewish jinnia. In the former case, the Jews lacked the moral
and religious authority to rid the girl of the jinn, while in this case it is only
Ibrahim who has the power—in spite of the Israeli prison guards' obvious military power—to control this situation.

The fact that Ibrahim's jinnia is Jewish and female is as relevant as the fact
that Zahia's jinn was Jewish and male. Ibrahim's experiences with this jinnia—
a jinnia who is immoral, ugly, and, finally, subdued in her wishes and obedient
to Ibrahim—are suggestive of Ibrahim's sense of Jewish women and the roles
they may play in Palestinian men's lives. While Zahia's Jewish jinn attempted to
make her murder her infant son, Ibrahim's Jewish jinnia attempts to lure Ibrahim
into an inappropriate union. Such a "marriage" would presumably severely
threaten his social standing in his village and attractiveness to a more appropriate mate. It would also clearly align him with an evil jinnia who is also a Jew, a
traitorous act at best. This seduction is successfully resisted by Ibrahim, who instead enters into a mutually productive friendship with her.

Further, the fact that Ibrahim's jinnia is both female and Jewish may reflect
a specific interpretation of Palestinian self-identity, based on the contrast between Israeli and Palestinian women. Jewish women may at times be seen as
temptresses, immoral in comparison to Palestinian women. While I have
mentioned village women's understandings of Jewish women, particularly
the way in which they contrast their own village social mores to those by
which Jewish women are purported to live, here we see that men, too, may at
times draw similar moral contrasts and affirmations of identity. Crapanzano
argues that the spirit often represents what its human host is not; thus,

> Possession appears to collapse at least temporarily the defining other—the
> spirit's carrier—by which the other is constituted in a dialectic of identity
> formation. . . . That such a dialectic often involves possession by spirits of a
> sexual identity opposite to that of the carrier reflects the fact that 'male' and
> 'female' are very potent symbols of otherness in identity formation. (1977a: 19)

In the case of Ibrahim and others discussed here, not only is the sexual identity of the spirit a key symbol of "otherness" for Ibrahim, but so, too, is the
spirit's religious identity. Ibrahim further refuses her as his wife, denying her
the status of an appropriate mate. Ibrahim may be at the whim and mercy of
his Jewish Israeli prison guards—indeed, he may be significantly emascu-
lated by his years of imprisonment—but not at the hands of the Jewish jinnia.
Through his interactions with her he clearly establishes himself as an inde-

pendent, moral, Palestinian man who will not immorally align himself with an evil, Jewish jinnia.

The two—Ibrahim and the Jewish jinnia—may be opposed to one another in terms of identity, but they overcome these differences and become friends on Ibrahim's terms and not those of the jinnia. As friends, indeed as metaphorical siblings, they together entertain the other prisoners. The friendship is suggestive of a real possibility, albeit an unlikely one. Ibrahim, by persuading the jinnia to enter into a friendship with him instead of the kind of relationship she desired, establishes a reciprocally beneficial relationship with her. Here we are led to ponder how social geography—in this case the possibilities of proximity in particular—works for a human male Palestinian and a female Jewish jinnia, and, therefore, the implicit possibilities for relations between Palestinians and Jews.

Ibrahim's experiences with the spirit become a force for his empowerment and a force for his own sense of self-definition and identification. Notably, however, the influence of the jinnia is not so great as to cause Ibrahim's release. The power structure in prison may be reversed momentarily, but its structure remains intact.

NUR

Nur's story of the jinn in an Israeli prison differs in several ways from Hamid's and Ibrahim's. I met Nur at the Israeli-Palestinian Rapproachment Center in Beit Safafa. He told me this story when I told him about my research interests in the jinn:

> In 1988 I was 16 and in jail. All the younger boys were kept in one room together in the jail. We were about twenty. One day, a Friday, the soldiers were baking chickens just outside our cell. All of us wanted a chicken badly [this is a well-known technique used by the Israelis—baking chickens near the prisoners' cells, throwing parties where the prisoners can see, etc.]. A little while later one of the boys thought he heard a cat outside the cell. A few hours later, at around eleven, one of the boys went to the rubbish bin that was kept in the cell next to the toilet and took out a can. He began screaming that the can was actually a cat that was a jinn. The other boys in the room were very scared. A different boy then began saying that a pair of slippers were walking by themselves—that it must be a jinn walking in them. Another boy then began screaming that the Qu'ran was shaking by itself, again due to a jinn. Another boy said that a bucket was flying around the room. I tried to persuade the boys that they were imagining it, even though I myself was very afraid. I told them that I wanted to use the toilet but the other boys tried to persuade me not to; they said the jinn were living in the bathroom. So, because I am a Christian, I crossed myself and then went to the bathroom, showed them the can from the rubbish, walked in the slippers, and held the

Qu'ran. But there was one boy from Ramallah who began to say that I could control the jinn, that I had a connection to the jinn. All the other boys began to avoid
me, refuse to speak to me, or deal with me in any way.

Two days later, thank God, I was released, or else I don't know what would
have happened to me there. Those two days, between the incident and when I
was released, were very difficult for me.

I really didn't understand how they could behave like that. Some of the boys
were even members of the PFLP [Popular Front for the Liberation of Pales-
tine]—so how could they believe in the jinn? I mean, how could they say they
are Marxists and still believe in such things?

While in their prison cell, the fears of the young boys, exacerbated by the
cruel techniques of the Israeli guards, created the grounds for an attack by the
jinn, who moved things about the room uncontrollably. Nur tried to show the
boys that their fears were ungrounded, but to no avail. This story reinforces
certain themes already discussed, particularly the emphasis on prison as a
place of fear and dirtiness (both symbolically and literally), factors that contribute to prisoners' particular susceptibility to attack by the jinn.

Important in this story, however, is Nur's Christian background that did not
allow for beliefs in the Muslim jinn. It is interesting to note that he criticized
the young boys who believed the slippers and the can to be possessed by the
jinn on the grounds that they considered themselves to be Marxists and members of political parties, not explicitly because of their Islamic religious beliefs. Yet he is suggesting that to be politically informed and Marxist is to reject "superstition" such as beliefs in the jinn, and indeed, Islamic beliefs. His
story leads us to consider the kinds of tensions that exist between Muslims
and Christians in the West Bank and how these may come to the fore in the
cramped space of an Israeli prison cell. The other boys' accusations that Nur
himself controls the jinn and their avoidance of him during his remaining
days in prison leads us to consider the importance of religious beliefs and
identity in the creation of meaningful ties to others. Nur's rejection of
and seeming alliance with the jinn marked him as highly suspect in the eyes
of the other boys in the cell: He was not one of them.

"MY WIFE IS FROM THE JINN"

The final story of the jinn in an Israeli prison discussed here focuses on an
anonymously authored, serialized story titled "My Wife Is from the Jinn,"
which was published in the popular magazine *Fosta* in the West Bank. It
draws out in great detail many of the themes discussed above.[2] *Fosta*, a
monthly magazine published in Ramallah, is widely circulated in the West
Bank. According to *Fosta's* publishers, approximately 25,000 copies of the

magazine are sold each month, which may indicate an actual readership of approximately 75,000 to 100,000 for each monthly issue. The magazine is quite popular with young people in particular. It contains advertisements for clothing stores, regular features on love and marriage, and stories of popular interest. Generally sold alongside newspapers, *Fosta* resembles a tabloid and has a far more sensationalist tone than most newspapers.

This story, like Ibrahim's, begins in an Israeli prison, but then quickly moves to a village setting. The story is part of a widespread public and literate discourse on the jinn, as opposed to stories of the jinn that circulate orally among friends and family of the possessed in Artas. As such, it is a depersonalized story of a young man no one knows. Removed from an immediate, known village context, I found that the story invited its readers (or listeners) to make more explicit comparisons to their own lives than stories of the jinn that circulate in Artas about a particular person. This story thus provided an opportunity for young people who knew its details to draw more personal meanings from it than from those stories which are heard in Artas about Artasis.

An abbreviated version emphasizing only the highlights of the story is as follows:

> Hassan is a young man who, after studying abroad, decided to return to Palestine. Upon his return, he is immediately imprisoned by the Israelis. While in prison he catches his first glimpse of a beautiful jinnia. After his release from prison, the jinnia appears to him again and tells him that her name is Ghada.
>
> Ghada and Hassan quickly fall in love and decide to marry secretly, in the traditional way of the jinn. They do this in spite of the risks their marriage poses for Ghada in particular, who, if caught, will suffer severe punishment from the Katu, the rulers of the jinn world. After they marry in a private ceremony, they spend time together in a paradise-like place which is part of the jinn world. They realize while in this garden of paradise, however, they are being constantly watched by black cats, helpers for the Katu. They flee to the human world, where Hassan must stay while Ghada continues to flee from the Katu who always hunt her.
>
> Ghada continues to visit Hassan, who is increasingly socially isolated from his family and village. One day Hassan meets an old man named Omar, who explains that he is actually quite young, but because of the evil influence of a jinnia named Ghada he has aged unusually quickly. Hassan is persuaded that the jinnia who did this to Omar must be his own beloved Ghada; Hassan thus severs his connection to Ghada immediately. Ghada, abandoned by Hassan, is quickly arrested and imprisoned by the Katu.
>
> One day a jinnia who looks like Ghada appears to Hassan, threatening him. Hassan returns to Omar, hoping for an explanation, only to hear Omar triumphantly exclaim that he works for the Katu and had successfully duped Hassan. The jinnia who looks like Ghada reappears to Hassan, explaining that her name is Marah and that she will make him suffer as Ghada is suffering in the prison of the Katu. We further learn that Marah is Ghada's sister. To prove her

strength, Marah makes Hassan appear the fool when he and his family go to the
home of one of Hassan's female relatives to (unsuccessfully) become engaged
to her. Marah then tells Hassan she will help him free Ghada, but he must first
pass a series of tests.

Hassan begins to desire Marah in spite of her evil and mean ways (and the
fact that she is his wife's sister); Marah eventually seduces Hassan. When Marah
appears next to Hassan she offers him a choice: he can have Ghada come back
to him or he can go through the gates of the jinn world, which, should he pass
through them, would grant him great wealth. Hassan chooses to go through the
gates and leave his village.

[Pictures of Ghada and Marah are sprinkled throughout each issue's story.
Claudia Schiffer and other famous American models are shown as one or the
other jinnia, often interchangeably. Even when not blonde and blue-eyed, the
models are always white skinned and dressed in revealing clothing.]

Diaspora and Return

Although the magazine provides neither pictures nor a description of his appearance, Hassan, at least initially, is a familiar character to many villagers:
He spent time in the diaspora but missed his family and decided to return
home. As has been true for so many others, his return was not entirely easy.
Hassan was imprisoned by the Israelis the moment he stepped off the plane;
when released he had difficulties adjusting to village life. Returnees from the
diaspora are well known to have difficulties in adjusting and fitting into
the social life of their villages and in accepting the realities of Israeli occupation and infiltration into Palestinian life (cf. Dennis 1998; Kanafani 1995;
Khader 1997; Khalidi 1995; Tamari and Hammami 1998). Hassan's plight as
an out-of-place returnee in village life is unmistakable, highlighted by his
entrance into the jinn world. Hassan's entry into the world of the jinn may
be seen as an escape from normal village life, as well as a subtle commentary on the difficulties associated with reentering village life from the diaspora.

It quickly becomes clear that Hassan is a lonely and socially isolated character in the village; he mentions no human friends and relies only on his sister for occasional help and understanding. While Hassan claims in an early
episode that he had begun to fit back into village life (April 1994), a sentence
later he tells us that Ghada first appeared to him while he was alone in his
room while his family was attending a wedding in the village. It is very
strange indeed for a young man of marriageable age in a village to prefer to
stay at home alone as Hassan does instead of going to a wedding. Spending
time alone in general is usually frowned upon (and, indeed, seen as a dangerous opportunity for the jinn to attack). It is presumed that socializing with

others is always preferable. Time spent alone is also seen as a luxury and thus rarely permitted by the demands of a young man's family. In Artas, young men are not allowed to disappear without explanation for long periods of time (as Hassan does), nor given the freedom to spend hours in daydreams while at home (which Hassan also does). Their families rely on them for earning a wage and building their homes.

It is well known, however, that the exceptions to these rules are the few villagers who have spent most of their lives abroad and have recently returned to Artas (and, of course, the physically or mentally unwell). Often returnees have earned enough money to support themselves for long periods of time in the village without working full-time. They may also choose to be alone rather than to socialize with others in the village, having lost their sense of belonging in the village because of the distance and time apart from their extended families. Further, their exposure to, and possible adoption of, alternative lifestyles and desires sets them apart from, and morally suspect to, other villagers, contributing to the returnees' sense of unease.

The fact that Hassan is an out-of-place returnee may explain not only his isolation and loneliness in village life, but may also be the source of at least some of his moral failings. Villagers who read the story wonder if Hassan's moral failings as a man and a husband (discussed further below) are due to his time away from his village, time spent in the diaspora. Hassan's shortcomings may be seen as reminders of the potential moral failings of those who grow up in places lacking the strict moral code of village life. We may see some of these effects on Hassan: he is a tortured character, filled with self-doubt, and given to fits of child-like anger. Hassan demands to know the "truth" from the jinn characters who enter his life and is always dissatisfied by their indirect answers. In many matters, Hassan is weak, unable to make difficult decisions; he is decisive only after being pushed to make a decision by a wound to his pride. While under the influence of Marah, Hassan expresses his refusal to marry his relative through an undignified practical joke on her and her family, thereby indicating his (albeit due to the influence of the jinnia) rejection of village social patterns. Hassan also reveals his greedy nature (seen in his longing to possess the gold shown to him by Ghada in the world of the jinn (December 1994) and his decision to traverse the Gates of Evil instead of having Ghada return to him (July 1997)). Greed is an undesirable trait in a man and is grounds for attack by the jinn. Further, Hassan lacks a well developed ability to carefully consider his responsibilities to others and act on those duties. As with a young village child, Hassan's ability to practice social relations properly is lacking. Hassan, in sum, is not very "manly."

Hassan is also a sad figure as a husband to Ghada. He is weak before her, deserts her on account of persuasion by another jinn (April 1995), and carries out acts of infidelity with her sister (November 1995). In contrast, most husbands in Artas believe that it is their responsibility to bring home a wage that supports their families and to deal with their wives and children in moderate and moral ways that are firm without being harsh, but that clearly point to their role in establishing limits on their family members' behavior. Thus husbands will generally decide whether or not their wives may work outside the house, and most women will feel obliged to abide by their decisions. In many other instances, husbands and wives negotiate decisions pertaining to their homes and children. Hassan is unable to accept his responsibilities as a husband to a human wife in the village.

Hassan thus has the traits of a failed husband, which may not be so uncommon in daily life for villagers, but are rarely discussed outright. Hassan's status as both a returnee and as a man involved with the jinn may allow for the articulation of these sentiments. In a close-knit village, a woman's neighbors may be well aware of her husband's misguided actions (as they are of hers), but neighbors generally attempt to minimize the importance of these failings in daily practice. Yet in both the world of the jinn and within his village as an outsider, there is only momentary escape from the eyes of others for Hassan—in the jinn world the Katu are omnipresent, as the jinn and one's neighbors are similarly present in village life. Thus Hassan's failures are known to the members of the jinn world but, unlike villagers in their dealings with one another, the jinn do not "pretend not to see" his shortcomings.

The effects of the diaspora are seen not only in Hassan's loneliness or in his status as a morally suspect outsider. When family members, including husbands and wives, are separate for long periods of time, their emotional ties to one another may weaken. Most villagers now have loved ones who have lived for years in the diaspora. Maintaining feelings of closeness is often difficult, although faraway family members are loved and missed. Further, villagers are often deeply disappointed that many family members are unable to—or, indeed, choose not to—return to those who love them in the village.

The deleterious consequences of distance for social relations emerge clearly in Hassan's tale: Hassan's love for and marriage to Ghada following their separation is quickly replaced as a central theme by his illicit desire for Marah, who claims to be Ghada's sister. Marah's success in seducing Hassan—and Hassan's weakness in the face of Marah's determination—are in part due to the fact that Ghada is far away (imprisoned by the Katu), confirming the importance of proximity for maintaining appropriate social relationships. In village life it is rare to have the potentially dangerous consequences of separation so explicitly expressed as they are in Hassan's story; here again, Hassan's story of the jinn speaks to what is generally not spoken of directly.

In sum, Hassan is a selfish man who exercises neither his rights nor his responsibilities in village life and fails in his roles of son and husband. Why Ghada and Marah continue to be drawn to Hassan in spite of their knowledge of his obvious shortcomings is unclear. Ironically, Hassan's imprisonment, which led to his involvement with Ghada and the jinn world, stems from his selfless decision to return to Palestine; presumably, Hassan, like many young Palestinian men in the diaspora, would not have needed to return. The fact that Hassan does return speaks to his sense of responsibility and a sense of national fidelity. Yet these sentiments are not enough.

Love and Desire

Notions of romantic love abound in Artas. Artasis, like villagers throughout the West Bank, watch *The Bold and the Beautiful* (an American "soap opera") daily (except during Ramadan when the Jordanian channel where it usually appears does not carry it). Westernized ideas of romance—of choosing one's mate (preferably a handsome stranger), dramatically falling in love, and being "swept away"—are commonly discussed by young people. Hassan's story addresses notions of love and desire that cross group boundaries and lead to faraway and unknown places. In contrast, in Artas, the majority of young people marry within the village; if a young woman is sent away to marry she is often fearful for her future happiness, as she will live far from those with whom she has grown up and whom she knows best.

The fact that Hassan fell in love with and decided to marry Ghada, a stranger to village life, foregoing all of the village practices typically associated with marriage, has numerous repercussions: Ghada is imprisoned by the Katu; Hassan loses his beloved Ghada; Hassan and his family are talked about by the people in the village who have heard rumors of Hassan's involvement with the jinn and stopped coming to Hassan's home (January 1995); Hassan is tortured by the lure of Marah and the Gates of Evil. In short, Hassan's marriage to his jinnia wife is a bankrupt decision, except for the few moments of happiness he and Ghada shared when they first married (November 1994).

What was the lure of Ghada for Hassan? Ghada is shown in many pictures in *Fosta*. She is beautiful and is often pictured with long black hair (although she is sometimes seen as blonde), and always with white skin and large eyes. She is tall and slim and usually wears revealing clothing. Ghada is also bold, visiting Hassan when he is alone in his room and agreeing to marry him when she knew the risks this would pose for her. She is vulnerable to Hassan's doubts that the jinn truly exist and she refuses to state directly that she is from the world of the jinn.

Yet Ghada in some ways is not so unlike village women. After all, Ghada is a principled character who sees herself as living according to her principles. It is the specifics of her morals which often, but not always, differ from those of Artāsi women. For example, Ghada will not sleep with Hassan until he marries her, she refuses to allow Hassan to kill and eat a rabbit from the world of the jinn (a selfish act, in her opinion), and she always keeps her promises. Further, Ghada is honest and does not spare her words when she comments on the weaknesses and downfalls of humans, at times chiding Hassan for his stupidity and selfishness—characteristics, in Ghada's opinion, of most humans. Ghada, like village women, restricts who may see her, appearing only to Hassan among all humans because she feels that she can trust him. Although issues including fertility and a moral "cleanliness" are central to women's lives in Artas for establishing themselves as morally upright, for Ghada these issues of morality are peripheral (neither she nor Hassan discuss children, and such mundane matters as housework are of no relevance in the story).

Ghada is an exotic and foreign being to Hassan. She is more tempting, more beautiful, and more difficult to figure out than any women he has ever known. In spite of Ghada's similarities in some ways to village women, it is her foreign qualities which make her so desirable to Hassan. Yet these same qualities make it difficult for Hassan to trust her completely; he episodically doubts her until he finally foregoes her presence completely as a result of the persuasion of the jinn Omar.

These foreign qualities may suggest that Ghada is symbolic of not only foreign women for the readers of *Fosta*, but Israeli women in particular. In considering the likeness of Ghada to Israeli women, an important point to be considered is Hassan's knowledge of Hebrew, which was highlighted by my discussants as significant. This point underscores the context of Hassan's love affairs in their political context of Israeli occupation. It is when Hassan is in the hospital for his paralysis (May 1994) that we learn that Hassan speaks Hebrew "very well," although the source of this knowledge is not explained. Speaking Hebrew is a key symbol for men of economic capital. It is proof that they have worked inside Israel, earned a good wage, and were able to "figure out" Hebrew. Women, however, often view the acquisition of Hebrew with distrust and feel that it may be symbolic of a moral transgression. Thus Hassan's fluency in Hebrew strikes a familiar note with his readers—he knows Israeli ways and is not impervious to the moral dilemmas such familiarity often fosters. It is in this context that we must frame his affair with Ghada and, indeed, Marah.

In addition, while distance pulled Hassan and Ghada apart emotionally, as it may draw apart villagers from their loved ones in diaspora, it is also important to recall that it was proximity on Israeli-controlled territory which brought them together: Ghada was attracted to Hassan because he, like her, loved the tree present in the courtyard of the prison where Hassan was held (Ghada found the tree when lost as a child and continued to visit it). Their love was the result of their chance meeting in this place, although they are members of different peoples. Thus Hassan's imprisonment by those with whom he and his family are in close proximity stands in contrast with his experience of falling in love with a jinnia with whom he also shares a space: The possibilities (ranging from persecution to love) for social relations entailed by proximity are made vivid here. Indeed, it is interesting to note that Hassan becomes so attached to the other prisoners and seeing Ghada that he did not want to leave the prison (April 1994), further demonstrating the possibilities for forming meaningful and deep friendships which stem from proximity.

Like Ghada, Marah is foreign, but, unlike Ghada, she is the kind of foreigner to be feared and dreaded. Marah is mean and unable to be trusted. It is ironic that she appears to be identical to Ghada, for the resemblance is only skin deep. The comparison of Ghada and Marah (foreign sisters who physically resemble one another), speaks to both Palestinian men's and women's impressions in the West Bank of foreign—and in particular Israeli—women, impressions which tend to be extreme. Kind and principled or evil and immoral, foreigners are a constant part of life in the West Bank—they are always nearby—and they infiltrate the moral consciousness of Palestinians in important ways.

More specifically, however, Marah, as the explicit embodiment of anti-virtue and an immoral temptress, is comparable to village women's perceptions of Israeli women's "loose" ways. Yet the actual exploits of Israeli women are rarely articulated in detail by village women. Here, in Marah's case, we know exactly what she does. This detailed articulation of Marah's evil acts speaks again to jinn stories as vehicles for social critique, expressing what is otherwise left unsaid, or spoken of indirectly. Human parallels of Marah—women who are mean and immoral—exist for villagers in daily life. Such women may be Israelis or even women from the village (but always in a faraway neighborhood). These women, Israeli or Artasi, are the subjects of gossip, their reputations dirtied by the fact that stories about them are publicly known and discussed (whether or not the gossip is true).

Is Hassan's story thus a moral lesson in the dangers of marrying a woman one does not know well and, in particular, risking involvement with Israeli women? Quite possibly. Perhaps if Hassan had not been so easily swayed by the lies of the jinn Omar (March 1995) and had been more convinced of Ghada's goodness, the story might have turned out differently, focusing our attention on Hassan's qualities as a man rather than on his decision to marry a jinnia and, indeed, on the potentially positive qualities of foreign women. Yet the dangers of the jinn world, symbolic as they are of the dangers posed by the foreign and particularly Israeli world, are nonetheless clear in the story and cannot be taken lightly. Their opportunity to be close to one another in the prison courtyard may have drawn Hassan and Ghada together, under the externally imposed conditions of imprisonment for Hassan. This situation should be compared to the circumstances of other men who have experiences with the jinn while in prison: Hassan's involvement with Ghada is a signal of his social displacement, of the experience of power to which Hassan is subject.

Further, Hassan's rejection of village life and practices (and the villagers' rejection of Hassan), coupled with the Katu's refusal to accept Hassan into the jinn world, leave the couple with nowhere to go. While the love between Ghada and Hassan may not in itself be an immoral experience, the fact that neither the community of the jinn nor Hassan's village offers the couple a place to live forces the conclusion that the possibilities of proximity, in this case, are limited. Hassan's story may be a lesson that romantic love is an empty choice if it forecloses opportunities to participate in the community or to have a place in village life, an interpretation that focuses our attention not on prescribed preferential marriage rules but on the practices (public performance and the work of maintaining a place in society) that surround and bolster a marriage.

In addition, if television shows such as *The Bold and the Beautiful* inform some villagers' ideas of romantic love, then Hassan's affair with his wife's sister is evidence that he is living through an experience very much like an episode of the soap opera. While romance with a stranger may seem to be an exciting possibility to young people, it is framed by the dangers not only of losing one's place in the village but also of implicating oneself in meaningless affairs with people who do not care about the appropriate responsibilities of an individual who is part of a social network. Thus the young people with whom I watched *The Bold and the Beautiful* in Artas both giggled over the twists and turns of the characters' love affairs and shook their heads at the ease with which the unions were formed and broken. Social relationships are nurtured carefully in Artas, maintained through daily acts of reciprocity and respect, and controlled through gossip and other acts of honor maintenance. Cutting off a social relationship or treating it with disrespect is a carefully considered decision and, indeed, may not be allowed by those surrounding the individual.

Hassan, having entered the world of the jinn through his marriage and involvement with the cast of jinn characters, is outside the realm of village practices that both protect and control individuals' behaviors. Hassan's affair with Marah and its obvious hurtful implications for his relationship with Ghada, as well as the comment it makes on the weakness of his character as an honorable man and dutiful husband, speaks to the dangers of falling in love with a stranger and disregarding village social mores. Foreigners have affairs while married and pursue other dishonorable activities; villagers should be wary of such people and their actions, for they contain little satisfaction. Ultimately, therefore, this experience of love speaks powerfully to the maintenance of social boundaries and the idea that proximity is not necessarily enough to create the grounds for appropriate relationships.

The contrast of these experiences of romantic love with those Hassan experiences with his mother and sister is dramatic. Hassan's mother and sister are concerned for Hassan's health, worry about him, and suffer on account of his suffering. His mother visits sheikh after sheikh in order to help Hassan, but to no avail (and doctors are equally useless). Indeed, the unfortunate woman is simply cheated out of her money when she is persuaded to purchase useless amulets and charms. Hassan's mother is fearful of the jinnia whom she believes has possessed Hassan, while his sister is enthralled by the details of the romance. Hassan's sister is, albeit only temporarily, his confidante, able to be trusted with important information. These two human women are the only characters of Hassan's family we get to know, and then only briefly. Both hope to arrange a marriage for him in order to make him happy, and both make excuses for him to protect him from gossip by villagers who do not understand his strange behavior.

Mother and sister are close to Hassan as they all live together in the family home, but they do not really know him, a fact that is intrinsic to the nature of social relations. Yet their love for Hassan is reliable. Hassan, however, largely overlooks their love, brushing it aside in favor of his own desires for Ghada and his involvement in the world of the jinn. The love of Hassan's mother and sister, enduring and selfless, is devalued by Hassan, who is seduced by the foreign ways and spirits of the jinn world. Compared to the complicated emotions Hassan has for Ghada and Marah, his feelings of affection for his mother and sister are straightforward, but lack the immediacy and compelling nature of his feelings for the spirits. Human women, such as Hassan's mother, sister, or, indeed, the generic "relative" whom Hassan was supposed to marry, are bland if morally righteous when compared to the jinnias.

As a wide-ranging social commentary, "My Wife Is from the Jinn," points to issues of importance to young men in particular in the West Bank, and provides another perspective on morality and villagers' relations to Jews.

MUHAMMED'S TWO WIVES

During the last few months of my fieldwork, *Fosta* published a short "news" feature, "Gazan Man Brings Together His Arab Wife and His Jewish Lover and the Children from Each of Them" (June 1996) in the place of one month's episode of "My Wife Is from the Jinn." The place of this story in lieu of the story of the jinnia and Hassan suggests that the editors of *Fosta* saw the two stories as speaking to similar issues and audiences.

The translated text of the story is as follows (translation is mine):

Every morning when Muhammed comes to his girlfriend's house in Tel Aviv, he helps her prepare the children to go to school, and then he goes to his job in construction. Every evening he passes the checkpoint to go to his wife and their children in Gaza. The strangest thing is the love between the two wives. Elza, the Israeli, says: "I visited the wife of my boyfriend. She is not my enemy, in fact she is my friend. She visited me here and I visited her there. It was an interesting meeting. She suggested that I should come and live with them." Muhammed said, "There is no reason for jealousy. I never lied to either of them. I am connected to both of them and I am the father of all the children."

After two months of the recent closure, the man from Gaza was in Tel Aviv and he sat for three hours in the kitchen of the apartment with a small Israeli girl and a boy, about 20 months old. "This is my dad," the boy said in Hebrew, while his father cried and cried. His father said, "I feel torn. I was saying to myself that I don't want to disappoint my children, but I am at the same time missing my children in Gaza. Whenever there is a closure in Gaza, I hope for a permission just once a week to see my children here in Tel Aviv and know that they are ok."

This is a rare story of love between two women, one Israeli and the other Palestinian. The source of the love is their love for the same man, Muhammed from Gaza. The legal wife of Muhammed is Laila, 43 years old, from Gaza, the mother of four boys, the youngest is two years old and the oldest is eight. His other wife is Elza, 36, from Tel Aviv and has two children, a girl and a boy. This has been going on for fifteen years. This assures us that nothing can stop love, not even the checkpoint.

Three normal people live together in peace and love. Every day since the closure Elza phones Laila and Muhammed. The two women discuss normal matters, their children, and Muhammed, and not one word about politics, not even security matters. Elza said, "We don't want to hurt each other and politics is harmful." Each is on one side of the conflict.

When there is no closure, Muhammed goes every day to Tel Aviv to see Elza and the children and send them to school and then go to his work at 8:30, after an hour with his family there. For 26 years he has been working inside the green line, except during closures and when there is curfew. And every evening he goes to his wife and children in Gaza. He would stamp his magnetic card at the checkpoint and then wait to meet Elza and their children the next day. Elza said, "When there are terrorist operations I would be very sad because I knew the children would not see their father until after the closure. And the children would ask and ask for him."

Elza was twenty-one when she met Muhammed. She was a romantic girl, dreaming about love. But she didn't expect to fall in love with an Arab man. "I grew up and heard from my family that you can't trust Arabs. I didn't expect to fall in love with an Arab man who is married and has children. But at that time I was a young girl and I came to Tel Aviv from Netanya to work as a cook. I rented a house in the south of the city. This man was living far away in a rented room. He used to come to this room to sleep with the other men working in

Gaza. Every Saturday he would return to Gaza. I met him for the first time at a party of a friend of mine. He saw me, and I saw him. I was afraid to think about him, but we became friends. I was very attracted to him. He was a gentle man, knowing how to respect and deal with people. I didn't know many Jews like him. Immediately, without realizing it, I brought him back to my house. I was afraid of having a relationship with this Arab man. But the love was stronger [than this fear]. He was honest with me from the beginning. He told me that he is married and has children. But I didn't tell my mother, father, or brother about him [being an Arab], because his accent did not reveal that he was an Arab and also, he was very light. We were in our relationship for three years before my mother and brother found out that he was an Arab. My mother loved him a lot. She said, 'So what? I discovered that he is an Arab. How am I going to suddenly hate him?' But my brother has not talked to me until this day and thinks that it is a shame. My brother is not the only one who was shocked by this. Many dear friends left me. This was a strange situation, everything related to Arabs was scary, because there were Jewish women who were pregnant by Arab men and then the Arabs left them. They told me to leave him because he would leave me, that I couldn't trust him. Also, they tried to pressure him to break off everything with me. Once they burnt his car here in Tel Aviv. Once they left a note in the front of his car threatening to kill him if he didn't leave me."

But Muhammed didn't leave Elza. When Muhammed talked about his love for Elza, he laughed. In the beginning Elza thought Muhammed would be just for her. She thought that he would live with her inside the Green Line. But he always told her that he wouldn't leave his wife and children. He would also tell Elza that he wouldn't leave her. He told Laila the same thing. He used to say to Elza, "I promise that I respect both of you." He is doing this until this day.

Elza was pregnant in her third month when Muhammed brought his wife and children to Tel Aviv. He said, "Now is the time for the two of you to get to know each other. I am going to take the children on a trip to give you a chance to sit together and talk. When I return I will find you either hitting each other or you will be laughing." But when he returned he found them drinking coffee and happy.

This was the beginning of a real love story among the three of them. Elza said, "I remember when his wife was looking at me when I was wearing shorts while I was pregnant. I wasn't expecting her to come. From that moment, I tried hard to appear in front of Laila in a more respectable way, without shorts or even makeup. Sometimes I would meet Laila without doing anything to look nice at all because I didn't want Laila to be jealous of me. That night Muhammed, Laila and the children stayed and slept at my house. From that moment, when we would meet together we would sleep together and the children on the ground and Muhammed in the salon because he didn't want to bother either one of us. Recently, Laila and the children come to Tel Aviv a lot and we go on trips, either in the city to a festival or to the beach. Because of the closures, I am missing those days when Muhammed would come with the children and go to the beach and me and Laila would talk and gossip at the beach. Muhammed would look after the children. I also miss visiting Gaza; the last time I was there was four years ago." Laila said, "I feel bad that we can't meet nowadays. Now there are two checkpoints, one for the Israelis and one for the Palestinians."

Elza said, "It is fun for me to go to Gaza. I still remember how my heart would beat when I would pass the checkpoint with Muhammed. I would wear Arab clothes to pass the checkpoint with the children in the backseat. Laila keeps asking me to visit Gaza and spend the weekend there. One day Muhammed came to me and brought a gift with him from her."

While Hassan's story draws out the problematic aspects of a love affair between a Palestinian man and a nonmember of his community, the moral angles of temptation, weakness, community disapproval, and power are for the most part distinctly peripheral to this story.

In the story of Muhammed and Elza, the positive possibilities of proximity are drawn on to understand this story of a love triangle that lacks the usual jealousies or obvious possible difficulties. Muhammed works on a construction site in Israel—a morally problematic space for both Palestinian men and women, as discussed in chapter 4. Indeed, it is because Muhammed works inside Israel that he was able to meet Elza and develop a relationship with her, a direct result of their proximity. Muhammed and his children speak Hebrew, another morally problematic social practice. Muhammed can "pass" for an Israeli. Yet Muhammed is not portrayed as either a fool or a traitor here. Rather, he carefully balances the demands of his two families, unwilling to desert one for the other, thus demonstrating the strength of his own honor. Yet ideally, my friends in Artas agreed, Muhammed should have properly married Elza and made her his legal second wife; she also should have converted to Islam. Their marriage would have then been legal and morally correct, if unusual. Muhammed and Elza's lack of public performance of the proper religious and marriage rituals, therefore, marks them as suspect.

Elza is the "typical" Israeli girl: she lives far from her family, was able to take a lover, wears shorts and makeup (although she decides not to do this in front of Laila). Yet Laila, the mother of four boys, embraces Elza as a new member of the family. Elza's friends and brother try to persuade Elza to end her relationship with Muhammed, attempting to force Elza to adhere to dominant social mores, an action similar to the role one would expect neighbors in Artas to play. Yet in Muhammed's story, we find love and tranquility between the two women who should be, by all accounts, the least likely of friends. A kind of shared essence of womanhood—which makes possible their ability to be understanding of one another—is called on here. This point was hotly contested in discussions of the story with my friends in Artas. There was no way, my friends agreed, that the two women could have been friends so easily and quickly, although they could have been friends after some time—and if they had the opportunity to live nearby, again demonstrating the possibilities of proximity.

Elza and Laila, while not immune to the effects of checkpoints and closures, disregard politics in their relationship to one another; indeed, they do not discuss politics out of fear of hurting one another's feelings. Instead, they focus on how they relate to one another as women, mothers, and wives of the same man, an experience which my discussants thought was unrealistic because, they argued, the process would simply have taken longer than the story suggests. Laila does not hold Elza personally responsible for periods of closure, nor does Elza blame Laila for terrorist operations. Their refusal to generate blame or hatred between themselves for events beyond their immediate control allows their friendship to develop.

Muhammed's love triangle is, in some ways, a near-parody of "real life," a life in which the strength of community disapproval for such a love affair between a married Palestinian man and an Israeli woman would in all likelihood have overwhelmed the two. The story is a parody of real life because there are without a doubt checkpoints, identity cards, religions, and nationalisms, all of which create gulfs of difference (and bitter emotions) between the experience of being a woman in Tel Aviv who has a boyfriend, and being the mother of four in Gaza whose husband must rely on unstable work inside Israel to feed his family.

Yet there is a striking note of optimism in this story, a sense of the possibility of what good relations between closely located Israelis and Palestinians could entail. In Artas, marriages, while often arranged between two families who have shared proximity and familiarity in the past, are also sometimes arranged in order to legitimate the possibility for closeness in the future. From the viewpoint of Artasis, the marriage of Muhammed and Elza creates a context for future marriages between their children and their cousins, both Israeli and Palestinian. The potential network of future ties that Muhammed and Elza have created between their extended families and, indeed, their neighbors and friends, is immense.

Here we are taken "after Jew and Arab" (to borrow the phrase from Alcalay 1993) to the seemingly more simple world of men and women. This story of the divides, pressures, and restrictions of real life, echoed in less optimistic ways in rumors of what goes on between Israeli women and Palestinian men at construction sites, may provide a glimpse of where the imagination may go when intolerance fades or is challenged. There is the possibility of a tolerant ethic of neighborliness at one end of the spectrum and love and marriage at the other ("This assures us that nothing can stop love, not even the checkpoint," the author writes). Yet it is clear that this proximity may also create the potential ground for great moral danger.

* * *

Prison is an obvious and extreme problematic social space, symbolically and indeed physically aligned with places of dirt, immorality, and the presence of the jinn. Such an explicit alignment of the jinn and the prison space highlights how the moral evaluation of a particular space as problematic associates it with the jinn and should inform our reading of the locations of women's stories of the jinn as well. While Samira's story may point us to the obvious space of the bathroom, other women's stories of the jinn, such as Zahia's story which took place in her marital home, as well as Nura's and Halah's stories in the homes of their families, point to these spaces as problematic enough to encourage the presence of a jinn and as potentially morally problematic for women's lives as prison may be for men. Men's stories of the jinn and prison may be more explicit in their evaluation of these places as negative and at least potentially problematic; yet women's stories are revealing for what they tell us of the subtle ways in which spaces and relations that are meant to enclose and protect may be dangerous as well.

Men's stories of the jinn often direct attention to the range of ways in which experiencing contact with Jews is dangerous. Men's stories may reflect on illicit and/or immoral sexual and emotional unions with Jews or, more generally, foreign others; they may tell us of the threat posed by a young man giving up his place in village life for an alternative lifestyle. Women's stories of the jinn that I gathered did not broach these kinds of moral problems for themselves, but pointed to these possibilities for men and, stemming from these possibilities, some of the consequences for themselves. Indeed, a number of the jinn stories discussed here complement women's sense and/or knowledge of the multiple layers of threat posed by men's greater and more intimate exposure to Jewish Israelis discussed in previous chapters. Men do indeed experience more of these threats for themselves in their daily lives as they are both allowed and indeed, forced, through the requirement that men bring home a wage, to go further away from village life than women. Women's stories remind us that many people must live with the consequences of exposure to Jewish Israeli life—men and women alike.

Men's and women's stories of the jinn share other kinds of common ground, however, and should not be quickly dichotomized. Both address the importance of close relationships—their need for careful fostering and their potential to be harmful. Stories from both groups may be empowering as well as subversive, even if only temporarily, as well as supportive of the status quo. Women's stories may tell us about husbands, men's stories may reflect on appropriate wives; women's stories may suggest that they embrace key cultural ideals, such as fertility, while rejecting blame if they cannot measure up to these ideals; men's stories tell us that the total rejection of the moral practices of and relationships to others may not be easily accomplished.

NOTES

1. Ibrahim's description of the jinnia is in some ways reminiscent of tales of 'A'isha Qandisha, the jinnia she-devil found in Morocco (Crapanzano 1980). Lalla 'A'isha, or "Lady" 'A'isha, is camel-footed and vindictive and, in Crapanzano's biographical ethnography (1980), is married to and controls a man called Tuhami. Crapanzano describes Lalla 'A'isha:

> She could appear either as a hag—an archetypical phallic mother, with maenad-like curls, long pendulous breasts, and elongated nipples—or as a beauty with extraordinary seductive powers. She was, however, always a capricious, vindictive spirit, and she harshly controlled the lives of those men who succumbed to her. . . . The ultimate relationship was one of enslavement. (1980: 15)

In Morocco, curing one of a demon, or jinnia, must be done through a *hadra*, or trance-dance; in trance, the victim of the demon loses control. He may experience cataleptic seizures or mutilate himself (Crapanzano 1980: 19). When the victim has danced enough to satisfy the jinn, he eats, sleeps, and should awake cured (Crapanzano 1980: 19). Tuhami, however, never underwent the *hadra*, but instead had a long-lasting relationship with Lalla 'A'isha. Crapanzano argues that the jinnia allowed Tuhami "a radical shift of responsibility, of motivational locus, from self to Other, from who he is to who he is not" (Crapanzano 1980: 20). As a victim of the demons, Tuhami thus confronts neither "the ultimate horizon of fate" nor "the personal limit of individual initiative and enterprise" (Crapanzano 1980: 20).

2. The first episode of the story was published in April 1994 and continued throughout most of the following two years until July 1996. The story did not appear in the following issues: August 1994, October 1994, February 1995, May 1995, October 1995, February 1996, and June 1996. I gathered, translated, and discussed with young people from Artas and Bethlehem University all of the issues that contained the story during my fieldwork. At the time of my fieldwork, the story had not yet concluded, but there was a significant amount of material available to work with from these issues. I have not included a discussion here of issues that were published following my fieldwork as I have not had an opportunity to discuss them with Artasis or other Palestinians.

When I asked if it would be possible to interview the author of "My wife is from the jinn," the publishers of *Fosta* answered that the author's identity will be revealed in a press conference when the story reaches completion. Until that point, the author wishes to remain completely anonymous and will not grant interviews.

Chapter Six

Social Geography and the Jinn

The subordinate discourse of the jinn and the practices of social geography implicitly reveal both the social construction of central facets of village life—including family, village social space, morality, and the religious beliefs—and their power-laden, complex dimensions. What is typically taken for granted as "natural" or immutable "fact" is critiqued, probed, revealed, and challenged through these practices and beliefs. Here we may go past or, in a sense, behind the highly visible realms of street battles and stonethrowing and negotiating tables and news conferences, and into the intimate realms of daily life as experienced by many Palestinian villagers. These realms include those of home and prison, family and neighborly relations, the personal and familial repercussions of emigration, and the forced division between those outside and those within the West Bank. The complexity of village life and the powerful relationships that create it are informed by the political economy of Israeli occupation, shaped by Islamic belief and practice, and always responsive to women's and men's changing notions of propriety and morality.

FAMILY

The discourse of the jinn and the logic of social geography highlight the various constructions and deconstructions of notions of family at work in village life. Creating kin stems not only from the history, present, and future of marriages and births, but also from shared location, friendships, practices of neighborliness, and common interests. Tracing the logic and outcomes of social geography provides one avenue for examining the ways that villagers' social relationships are created and maintained, without assuming that the dominant discourse of the *ḥamūla*, the genealogically-defined extended family, is the most important, exclusive, or timeless (or precultural) source (cf. Yanagisako and Delaney 1995: 11) of such relationships. Without a doubt, village women use the dominant discourse of the *ḥamūla* at appropriate moments to describe their relationships to others. Yet it is often presumed in anthropological accounts of the Palestinian extended family that the roles and relationships as described by the discourse of the *ḥamūla*—as between mothers and daughters-in-law, or a husband's sister and his wife—are experienced by women as prescriptive, typical, and almost singularly central to their lives (e.g., Rosenfeld 1968; Haj 1992; Rubenberg 2001). This point of view emphasizes the discourse of the *ḥamūla* to the exclusion of other ways in which social relationships are created in practice (e.g., Ata 1986; Escribano 1987).

Early studies of the *ḥamūla* in Palestinian village life were often concerned with understanding the *ḥamūla* as a patrilineage based on a "blood" group (Rosenfeld 1964), on the one hand, or, on the other hand, as a class structure (Asad 1975; see also Nakhleh 1977). The differences between these points of view can be understood as stemming from an overreliance on, or denial of, the historical continuity of the *ḥamūla*. Correspondingly, the effects of the Jordanian and Israeli occupations in the West Bank are under- or over-emphasized, either through authors' silence about their effects on the structure of the *ḥamūla* or their assertion that the occupations have directly shaped the Palestinian family with little resistance. The result is that the political consequences of occupation on Palestinian village and family social structure are underestimated, or the role of the Palestinian peasantry in shaping their own lives is denied. Such studies focus on the *public expression* of the *ḥamūla*, an arena dominated by men, at the cost of overlooking women's practices and perspectives (see Rothenberg 1998-99 for an analysis of these and other issues raised in this literature).

While women in the *hāra*, or neighborhood may, like men, use the language of the *ḥamūla* to describe their relationships to one another—indeed, neighbors are often family members—they combine this perspective with the implicit logic of social geography. Although women will thus explicitly recite genealogies, their practices reflect a logic for women's daily relationships that is centrally shaped (although not wholly encapsulated) by the limitations and allowances of social geography. The geography of the *hāra* emerges as a central force in women's creation and maintenance of social relations, as does the force of personal preference. Indeed, if we do not look solely to genealogies to explain the practice of social relationships, we can recognize that formally reckoned genealogies are just one factor among many that assist us in understanding those relationships.

Deconstructing the assumption that human reproduction is always the central element of kinship or, indeed, of gender constructs more generally (Yanagisako and Collier 1987; MacCormack and Strathern 1980; Rosaldo and Lamphere 1974) is thus pursued through following the logic of social geography. Social geography shows us the ways in which women in particular create meaningful relationships that are not based on reproductive or "blood" relations; it also helps us recognize the impact of the political economy of the occupied territories and the impact of a long-term Palestinian diaspora community on women's families. These factors do not merely *affect* the Palestinian family: they *shape* it, and in turn, these factors are reshaped by villagers, in an unending cycle.

This book brings to the fore aspects of women's and men's practices that widen our understanding of their social world by rejecting the assumption that the *ḥamūla* is the sole directive of women's relations. The poverty of the expressly stated, formal discourse of genealogical family is revealed here. It is through a focus on discourse and on symbolic as well as practical knowledge—social geography and the jinn in this instance—that we may "seek rather than assume knowledge of the socially significant domains of relations in any particular society and what constitutes them" (Yanagisako and Collier 1987: 34).

While it is necessary to question the assumption that places the genealogical relationships of the *ḥamūla* before all others, it is also necessary to interrogate the implicit assumptions of social geography—close locations and the careful fostering of relations surely do not insure trouble-free close relations. Close relations, whether between kin or neighbors, should be supportive, honest, and helpful. Of course, these characteristics are not always observed in practice, and the schism between *what is* and *what should be* is often keenly felt and expressed through stories of the jinn.

For example, jinn stories that draw our attention to adult women who are not married comment on both their highly problematic, out-of-place status in the social geography of village life, and on the problematic interference of one's close relations that may have created or contributed to their problems. Unmarried women's experiences reveal a complex and sometimes oppressive side of the village social ethos that requires a woman to marry to be considered on the road to adulthood, as well as some of the dangerous aspects of "close" relations in the social geography of village life. Close relationships, even when chosen by individual preference and fostered through reciprocity and care, are potentially dangerous, as they leave one vulnerable to the unknowable and darker side of human nature.

SOCIAL SPACE

Jinn stories and the practice of social geography also contribute to our understanding of village space as socially constructed rather than physically obvious or outside the boundaries of cultural constructs. The social construction of village space is clear when we recognize that seemingly private space—an enclosed, empty room, for instance—is not private at all when it is shaped by a religious belief in spirits that are ever-present. At the same time, public space may not be considered public or provide the grounds for punishment for publicly known acts, if those acts were caused by a jinn.

The oft-discussed distinction between public versus private space (Rosaldo 1974), particularly in sex-segregated societies, is complicated here by religious beliefs. The fact that women have power that influences the public sphere associated with men (Nelson 1974) has been well demonstrated in Middle Eastern societies. The emphasis here is on beliefs about a spirit world that significantly influences the actions of women and men and calls into question the boundaries of the private and the public. Here the borders of the realms themselves are not simply porous, but erased. Private spaces are public spaces and public spaces may be seen as enclosed, outside the realm of regulated morality, when influenced by the jinn.

Honor, propriety, and piety are thus significant concerns, and not just because other people take note of them; the spirits are always watching. Samira's story tells us that even when far from the sight/site of neighbors and family, the jinn are omnipresent, constant guardians of proper moral practice who do not allow women to stray. This perspective recasts the discussion of public and private space as a largely meaningless divide: one is never in truly "private" space. All village space is space socially constructed with respect to religious belief.

MORALITY

Women's stories of the jinn often speak to the moral requirements that differently structure women's and men's lives. These moral dictates are embraced as "naturally" right as often as they may be challenged. For example, the experiences and difficulties of infertile women in Artas—an inability to achieve adult status, the threat of divorce, and a lack of personal fulfillment—are similar to those of many women in a variety of cultures throughout the Middle East (see, for example, Inhorn 1996). Stories of the jinn and their relationship to women's experiences of infertility draw out this range of experiences while drawing attention to the role and responsibility of the jinn that has caused the problem. In these stories the moral mandate of fertility is not questioned; rather the blame placed upon women for failing in its fulfillment is questioned.

Samira's experience with the jinn comments on some of the taken-for-granted practices that divide men's and women's lives in inequitable ways, such as men's greater opportunities for rest and religious practice compared to the unceasing demands of housework and childrearing for women. In this case, the assumption of men's greater freedom and, indeed, moral worth, when compared to women's, is questioned in the implicit parallels in Samira's story between the immoral jinn and fallible human men. Samira's story leads to a recognition of her awareness that the "natural" division of labor and men's presumed moral superiority are gendered constructions at best, and unfair dictates according to which women must live at worst.

While women's stories of the jinn often lead us to consider the ways in which the adherence to moral rules for women and men is difficult for women in particular, women's moral transgressions may not always be punished as people claim they will be in the dominant discourse of honor in village life. In the story of the young girl who loses her virginity to a jinn, we gain a dramatic insight into the practice of "cover-up" for one who crosses the line of correct behavior, a practice that is articulated through a story of the jinn by recasting blame away from the individual and onto the jinn. This practice is, in part, a warning that things are not always as they appear. While Samira's story tells us that private actions may be in fact public ones and thus subject to constant scrutiny, this story tell us how a publicly immoral act may be treated as largely invisible.

Experiences of social geography and the jinn widen the possibility for insight into men's morality. The popular story "My Wife Is from the Jinn," for example, through a detailed narration of a Palestinian man's love affair with a jinnia whom he met while in an Israeli prison, addresses the experiences of returning from the diaspora, falling in love with foreign women, and failing to meet the demands of daily life for Palestinian village men. Villagers in Artas interpreted the story in light of their own experiences — a central aspect of which is the fact that many men in Artas are close to Israelis through their work building Israeli settlements both in the West Bank and inside Israel. The story suggests what many villagers believe — that the threat of Israel is not solely located in its military oppressiveness. Rather, Israel is implicated here in the ability of the foreigner to steal the heart of a young village man and persuade him to forego his place in his village. This disruption of the social fabric of village life is an inverse of the experience of "losing" one's daughter to an arranged stranger marriage. Women may leave the village, but the public backbone of the village is its young men. To lose such men to the lure of foreign ways is dangerous for the village as a whole, as well as for the young man in particular.

RELIGIOUS BELIEFS

Artasis were sometimes self-conscious about their jinn narrations, concerned that I would think that jinn stories were silly, foolish even, and, as a consequence, that I and my future readers would think the same of them. Similarly, in her study of Palestinian women's family planning practices in the Galilee,

Kanaaneh notes that people were very aware that her writings about them would "eventually travel in global circuits" (2002: 21). When Kanaaneh mentioned to a Palestinian in the Galilee some of the traditional practices women use to heal and protect their children, including those that protect children from the evil eye, he replied to her, "I hope you're not going to take those silly things with you and tell the Americans about them. That's not what you're doing, is it?" (2002: 21). Some might feel that is exactly the kind of endeavor I am engaged in here. During a year of postdoctoral research with the Palestinian community in Toronto, many Palestinians with whom I spoke were horrified by my dissertation topic, a few telling me forthrightly that I was making the Palestinians appear ignorant and backwards. This discomfort with jinn stories and where they fit within the Islamic repertoire of beliefs and practice is found in scholarly studies as well.

Indeed, echoing the sentiments in the comments of many of the Palestinians whom I met in Toronto are some scholars' studies of Islamic beliefs that have cast them in terms of the Great Tradition versus the Little Tradition: The tenets of Islamic texts—the "Great Tradition"—are typically compared to local practices—the "Little Tradition" (e.g., Gellner 1981; Antoun 1968; Abu-Zahra 1970; cf. Badone 1990). Some scholars may view jinn beliefs and stories as part of the Little Tradition, as they are related without significant textual elaboration and, to some, may seem to even stray from the realm of proper Islamic belief.

The Great and Little Tradition approach to Islamic beliefs and practices is intrinsically associated with the embrace of a problematic set of dichotomies understood to structure social life. As Tapper and Tapper (1987: 70) have eloquently argued, "Great is to Little as literate elite is to illiterate masses, urban is to rural, intellectual is to emotional, public to private, male to female, and so on." Jinn stories are at the intersections of each of these dualisms and certainly complicate the independent, bounded existence of any single one. Jinn stories are told and heard by illiterate women alongside literate ones. It is impossible to describe Artasis as rural when they are a few kilometers away from Bethlehem and a few additional kilometers away from Jerusalem, and when many men commute into these cities daily for work. The division of intellectual and emotional is certainly called into question by the knowledge and approach of Islamic curers who "operate" using both texts and great emotional force. The association of publicly acceptable knowledge and privately held, unacceptable knowledge, is untenable when an ongoing popular magazine sold at newsstands features a monthly story of a jinnia. Finally, told by both women and men, jinn stories belong to both, and it is simply incorrect to argue that jinn stories belong essentially to women.

Other scholars may see women's experiences with the jinn as examples of deprivation theory at work or as a by-product of domesticated religion. Deprivation theory argues that "people who are deprived of satisfaction in other areas of their lives turn to religion as compensation or as an outlet for their frustration" (Sered 1994: 62). I. M. Lewis has argued that women's participation in possession cults is an example of deprivation theory. In his view, possession cults are "thinly disguised protest movements directed against the dominant sex. They thus play a significant part in the sex-war in traditional societies and cultures where women lack more obvious and direct means for forwarding their aims" (1975: 31).

Jinn stories, as accounts of possession experiences, would, according to Lewis, constitute a means for achieving an end, whether that end is divorcing, staying married, shifting blame, or excusing an immoral action—any one of which is presumably contrary to what men would want. Deprivation theory is problematic in many respects; most centrally, "it places unwarranted emphasis on the assumed intentionality of women and thus insidiously underestimates the factuality of spirits" (Boddy 1989: 139). As Sered argues, the essence of the arguments of the proponents of this theory, who draw on cases of spirit possession as well as novel religious movements in America for their evidence, is "that women join religious groups for nonreligious motives" (1994: 65). The women discussed here would be presumed to be intentionally attempting to achieve a clearly defined goal—improved status—while the jinn would be the means for reaching the goal.

This reading of jinn stories is both limited and narrow. First, stories of the jinn often do not result in a change in a woman's status and, indeed, may reinforce aspects of women's lives: Samira's story is a case in point. Second, the jinn do not always work in women's favor—here again Samira's story is relevant. Yet even when a woman's life may be changed for the good because of the influence of a jinn, such as in the story of the young girl, her loss of virginity, and subsequent marriage, or Aliyah and her wish to remain married in spite of the couple's ongoing infertility, to argue that their stories of the jinn were a means only for achieving these goals is to essentially call these women liars, a second point of criticism of deprivation theory. This I am completely unwilling to do.

Jinn stories are complex: they may create change in a woman's life or they may not; they may be critical of village social mores structuring women's lives and even tell us of their subversion; or they may demonstrate that women believe they must be ever-vigilant enactors of appropriate morality. They may in some cases be largely made up (such as the story discussed in chapter 2) or, as I argue, more commonly, they may be told with total conviction. It is difficult, therefore, to argue that jinn stories reflect simply on women's subordination (after all, women's jinn stories often reflect on how they want to fulfill their gendered roles) or empowerment, a dichotomous formulation for understanding women's lives in any case. Further, men may not be opposed to—indeed, they may more or less explicitly be supportive of—the outcomes of some scenarios structured by the influence of a jinn. Women's jinn stories are nuanced and sophisticated and deny us the ease of saying what they categorically "do," with the exception of noting that what they always do is tell us about these women's lives and their social world.

Finally, as Boddy points out, deprivation theory overlooks the "fact" of the spirits themselves. Women's beliefs in, experiences with, and stories of the jinn may be seen by some as a way to "domesticate" religious beliefs, "to reinterpret aspects of the dominant male religion in ways that they as women find meaningful" (Sered 1994: 64). Yet young men have jinn experiences, too. For them, jinn stories relate to a range of issues, including the Israeli prison context. The jinn and stories about them are within the purview of both women and men, telling us of a range of experiences that affect, if in unequal and uneven ways, their lives in both domestic and particularly un-domestic-like spaces. Perhaps most important, the jinn are recognized by these women and men as actors from a spiritual world confirmed by the Qu'ran and true for believers.

Stories of the jinn are thus not cultural productions based on ignorance, the products of women's subordination, or the results of a "backwards" lifestyle. Rather, jinn stories are a locally meaningful belief, informed by all the currents of our postmodern age: fractured families spread throughout diasporas, the flow of global media, transnational travel, and the intimate juxtapositioning of heterogeneous communities, to name only a few. It is clear that the jinn that exist today for those who do believe in them are modern spirits, attracted to prisoners, unmarried women, Jews, Palestinians, and others—modern-day actors in today's West Bank. The jinn are not, therefore, a maladapted group's recourse or symptomatic of an individual's inability to cope with change.[1] Rather, jinn stories speak to the issue of change itself, articulating how, indeed, individuals do cope with change, contradictory demands, and the threat of immorality. That jinn stories deny us the simplicity of "doing" one particular task or fitting easily into a single category of "type" of religious belief only speaks further to their ultimately postmodern, complex qualities.

POWER AND RESISTANCE

Jinn stories and the practices of social geography are remarkably far-reaching; they draw our attention to not only the socially constructed nature of kinship, morality, social space, and religion, but also to the power of dominant social mores and the critical insights of those seemingly on the social and, indeed, spatial periphery as well as those at the center of village life. These stories thus provide a subtle means of articulating and reflecting on the many dimensions of power in village life, including the relationship between conservative village social mores and Israeli control, the politics of diaspora and homeland, and village social networks. Jinn narrations often speak to the intertwining of various sources of power and their ability to seemingly collude, enforce one another, and overlap. Power, as experienced by women and men, becomes a thick, complex reality, difficult to neatly boil down to one single source.

Jinn stories and the commentaries they provide are reminiscent of a variety of forms of women's discourses that have been studied by feminist anthropologists, including oral poetry (Abu-Lughod 1986), spirit possession (Boddy 1989; Brown 1991; Ong 1987), and weaving practices (Messick 1987). Located in an unequal power relationship to one or more of the dominant gender, religious, political, and economic discourses of the societies in which they are found, these subjugated discourses reflect distinctly critical, modern, and power-sensitive perspectives on social life. Certainly stories of the jinn add to and enrich this ethnographic record.

Yet, by reflecting on multiple sources of power and oppression in the lives of villagers that are simultaneous, competing, and ever-shifting, jinn stories speak to the malleability and inventiveness of a subjugated discourse engaged in by both women and men. This adaptability and its utility for both genders set jinn narratives apart from many other subordinate discourses in which only women typically engage. Power is not experienced identically by the genders; this divergence is reflected in the different kinds of stories of the jinn that women and men relate. The fact that both women and men nonetheless use narratives of the jinn reflects on the remarkable range and reach of this shared discourse.

Many men's stories, while not wholly unlike women's, demonstrate how men's experiences with the jinn are most often immediately associated with explicit conditions of intense oppression and control, such as torture and imprisonment. These stories remind us to look carefully at the sites that the jinn inhabit as sites of power; women's domestically-based stories of the jinn thus become even more charged with meaning. Men's stories also tell us of the lure of certain aspects of Israeli life and sexuality. These stories, when juxtaposed to women's, further our understanding of stories of the jinn as commentaries on power. Men's and women's experiences of power differ in village life, and so do the styles of their stories of the jinn. Women, who are perhaps more complexly and precariously entangled in webs of power than men, articulate through jinn stories many subtle messages about husbands, families, and their male relations' involvement with Israelis, as well as the requirements of morality. Men, often more physically at risk from the occupation but more secure in their standing in their families and communities than many women, tell us through their stories of the jinn of immediate bodily and moral threats to their well-being including, perhaps surprisingly, the threat of temptation by Israeli ways and women.

Because they tell us about power, it is tempting to "read" stories of the jinn as evidence of resistance. Yet it seems clear to me that jinn stories, while often expressions of degrees of resistance, are also reminders of the danger of romanticizing resistance (Abu-Lughod 1990). Few villagers have illusions about their own degree of power, although they are certainly not hopeless or passive. They know they may be capable of political revolution, but a man in prison or a woman caught in an unwanted marriage is subject to the experience of power with limited recourse. Their stories of the jinn may reflect moments of resistance to this subjection; indeed, some recourse may be located in these villagers' ability to articulate, through their stories of the jinn, the workings of power in its most sophisticated and subtle forms.

Although this articulation does not change the Israeli state structure or patriarchal village practice, we cannot assume it is wholly without repercussions. The "articulatory potential" (Boddy 1989: 141) of jinn narratives creates a potential space for comment, criticism, and even debate about these experiences of power. Once articulated, these expressions are "cast within the world of meaning and may provide a basis for action" (Crapanzano 1977a: 10). Actions stemming from the influence of the jinn are hugely variable and unable to be characterized in a simple fashion; indeed, there may seem to be no obvious action at all directly attributable to a jinn story. But even in these cases, it is impossible to know what may come from the telling of a jinn story, what insight may be revealed, and what consequence may thus eventually flow forth. It is possible that the ability to identify and critique the forms of power to which an individual is subject through stories of the jinn may open a space for other kinds of action. I hope to have given voice and recognition to this potential here.

NOTE

1. Ashkanani (1991: 219–20) argues along these lines for women involved with the *zar* in Kuwait: "I suggest that a certain category of Kuwait women (now middle-aged) have been unprepared for the changes, are unable to cope with them and are thus the victims of the spectacular growth the country is undergoing. . . . The emotional distress and isolation which they feel in modern westernised Kuwait find expression and release in the world of zar."

Appendix

Marriages in Artas

Making a match for a young couple can range from a complicated and long process to a quick and easy arrangement. As Granqvist noted:

> A marriage is seldom contracted without all kinds of complications . . . although it is the grown-ups who arrange the matter, it is no less exciting and certainly less innocent than if two young people are left to come to an agreement themselves. Old disputes and old hates are roused again; quite other facts interfere and dominate; questions of principle bound up with the interests of the family play a more decisive role than the feelings of the young people for each other. The whole thing is on another plane, it is not so much an affair of the individual as an affair of the family. (1931: 52–53)

Once a marriage has been arranged, a young woman will become publicly visible at her engagement and later marriage celebrations. This is the first occasion for which it is appropriate that she be at the center of public attention and noticeably well-dressed and wearing makeup. Immediately prior to the engagement and wedding celebrations the bride and groom will often go to particularly nice places to have their picture taken, including local churches and parks for an artistic backdrop. For their first pictures ever taken together, they will hold hands and artfully lean against one another. These pictures are widely distributed and the process of taking the photos is videotaped and included in the now inevitable wedding video. Interspersed between the photos of the carefully posed bride and groom are always pictures of waterfalls, flowers, and greenery, obvious symbols of fertility. This is the first step in increasing the bride's visibility. Often a family will hang an enlarged picture of the bride (the first publicly hung picture of her) in a room in the house.

At her engagement and marriage celebrations, a young woman will be seen wearing her white, Western-style wedding dress and heavy makeup. During most weddings men and women will dance and celebrate separately in the early part of the evening, men generally on a rooftop or courtyard, women in an enclosed large room. At times during the celebrations, different men closely related to the bride, including her brothers, father, and uncles, may enter the women's room to give the bride a gift of cash or jewelry and dance with the bride's mother. At the end of the evening of celebrating, when most of the guests have left, many close male family members will come into the women's room and all the relatives will dance together, husbands and wives often holding hands, surrounded by small groups of related cousins.

The practice of cousin, family, village, and stranger marriages (in terms of the dominant discourse on social relations) varies among different families, as seen below:

Types of Marriages in Artas, from the Perspective of the Dominant Discourse on Social Relations

Ḥamūla Name	Number of Marriages per Ḥamūla[a]	Percentage FBD (number of marriages)[b]	Percentage Other Family Members (number of marriages)[c]	Percentage Different Ḥamūla in the Village (number of marriages)[d]	Percentage Stranger Wives (number of marriages)[e]
Aish	104	7 % (7)	59 % (61)	11 % (12)	23 % (24)
Odah	87	17 (15)	45 (39)	17 (15)	21 (18)
Sma'in	78	19 (15)	44 (34)	32 (25)	5 (4)
Abu Swayy	71	21 (15)	25 (18)	34 (24)	20 (14)
Assad	47	19 (9)	30 (14)	32 (15)	19 (9)
Khalawi	44	11 (5)	34 (15)	27 (12)	27 (12)
Shahin	40	5 (2)	35 (14)	28 (11)	33 (13)
Sanad	25	36 (9)	44 (11)	8 (2)	12 (3)
Rabayya	26	23 (6)	27 (7)	31 (8)	19 (5)
Othman	13	15 (2)	46 (6)	31 (4)	8 (1)
Total	535	(85)	(219)	(128)	(103)
Average	54	16% (9)	41% (22)	24 % (13)	19% (10)
Granqvist's data[f]	264 (total marriages for village)	13.3%	20.4%	23.5%	42.8%

These data were gathered by Musa Sanad of Artas. The numbers were corrected and updated by my research assistant and me in 1996. The figures have been rounded to the nearest whole number.

A. This category refers to the total number of recorded marriages for a particular *hamūla* in the village.

B. FBD indicates a man's marriage to his father's brother's daughter.

C. "Family" here refers to extended relationships within the patronymic association (the *ḥamūla*).

D. "Village marriages" are those between two individuals from different *ḥamā'il* in Artās. As any number of possible genealogical links could be found between two such individuals, we followed Mr. Sanad's approach to grouping them together as "village marriages." This approach emphasizes a shared geographic proximity, from which many kinds of kin ties have followed.

E. "Stranger wives" are women from outside of Artas with no previous genealogical connection (or only a very distant one which has not been maintained) to the village.

F. Granqvist's data are found in her marriage tables (1931: 175–95). Only a partial family-by-family comparison between my data and Granqvist's is possible, as some family names have changed.

The percentage of first cousin patrilineal marriage in a single family ranges from 7 to 36 percent and does not correspond to the family's size. Incidence of first cousin patrilineal marriage may, however, correspond to other factors, such as a family's developmental cycle; this is a question for future research. Yet marriages among those considered to be family members (relations who range from cousins [not including the father's brother's daughter here] to much further removed) are in general far more common, ranging from 25 to 59 percent. It may be possible to theorize that other kinds of family relationships besides that of first patrilineal cousins are greatly valued, and that the value of these relationships may in large part depend on the degree of closeness, in both physical and symbolic terms, among family members. As H. Geertz argued for Morocco, "to center attention on this particular form of cousin marriage detracts from the much more important and pervasive pattern: marriage between close kinsmen of any sort" (1979: 325). This closeness cannot be assumed to follow a genealogical path, but rather may correspond to specific experiences of friendship and proximity.

Bibliography

Abu-Lughod, Lila. 1986. *Veiled Sentiments: Honor and Poetry in a Bedouin Society*. Los Angeles: University of California Press.
——. 1990. "The Romance of Resistance: Tracing Transformations of Power through Bedouin Women." *American Ethnologist* 17, no. 1: 41–55.
Abu-Zahra, Nadia M. 1970. "'On the Modesty of Women in Arab Villages': A Reply." *American Anthropologist* 72, no. 5: 1079–88.
Akin, David. 1996. "Local and Foreign Spirits in Kwaio, Solomon Islands." In *Spirits in Culture, History, and Mind*, ed. J. Mageo and A. Howard, 147–72. New York: Routledge.
Alcalay, Ammiel. 1993. *After Jews and Arabs: Remaking Levantine Culture*. Minneapolis: University of Minnesota Press.
Altorki, Soraya. 1986. *Women in Saudi Arabia: Ideology and Behavior among the Elite*. New York: Columbia University Press.
Altorki, Soraya, and Camillia Fawzi El-Solh. 1988. *Arab Women in the Field: Studying Your Own Society*. Syracuse, N.Y.: Syracuse University Press.
Anonymous. 1994–1996. Zaujatī min al-Jinn [My Wife Is From the Jinn]. *Fosta* [April, May, June, July, September, November, December 1994; January, March April, June, July, August, September, November, December 1995; January, February, March, April, May, July 1996].
Anonymous. 1996. Ghazāwī yujma'u baina zaujatihi al-'arabīyya wa-habībatihi al-yahūdiyya wa-aulādihi minhin [Gazan Man Brings Together His Arab Wife, His Jewish Girlfriend and His Children From Them]. *Fosta* (June): 58–59.
Antonosky, Helen, Mahmud Meari, and Judith Blanc. 1975. *Patterns of Socialization in an Arab Village*. Jerusalem: The Israel Institute for Applied Social Research.
Antoun, Richard. 1968. "On the Modesty of Women in Arab Muslim Villages: A Study in the Accommodation of Traditions." *American Anthropologist* 70, no. 4: 671–97.
——. 1972. *Arab Village: A Social Structural Study of a Transjordanian Peasant Community*. Bloomington: Indiana University Press.
Applied Research Institute–Jerusalem. 2003. February 10. Report about violated and confiscated lands in Artās village. http://www.poica.org/casestudies/Artas

Asad, Talal. 1975. "Anthropological Texts and Ideological Problems: An Analysis of Cohen on Arab Villages." *Economy and Society* 4, no. 3: 251–82.

Ashkanani, Zubayda. 1991. "Zar in a Changing World: Kuwait." In *Women's Medicine: The Zar-Bori Cult in Africa and Beyond*, ed. I. Lewis, A. Al-Safi, and S. Hurreiz, 219–29. Edinburgh: Edinburgh University Press.

Ata, Ibrahim Wade. 1986. *The West Bank Palestinian Family*. New York: KPI.

Ayoub, Millicent. 1959. "Parallel Cousin Marriage and Endogamy: A Study in Sociometry." *Southwestern Journal of Anthropology* 15, no. 1: 266–75.

Badone, Ellen. 1989. *The Appointed Hour: Death, Worldview, and Social Change in Brittany*. Berkeley: University of California Press.

———. 1990. Introduction to *Religious Orthodoxy and Popular Faith in European Society*, 3–23. Princeton: Princeton University Press.

Barghouti, Abdullatif. 1987. *Arab Folk Stories from Artas: Miss Crawfoot and Miss Baldensperger*. Bir Zeit: Bir Zeit University.

Barghouti, Mustafa. 1996. "Posteuphoria in Palestine." *Journal of Palestine Studies* XXV, no. 4: 87–96.

Barth, Frederick. 1954. "Father's Brother's Daughter Marriage in Kurdistan." *Southwestern Journal of Anthropology* 10, no. 1: 164–71.

Behar, Ruth, and Deborah A. Gordon. 1995. *Women Writing Culture*. Berkeley: University of California Press.

Boddy, Janice. 1989. *Wombs and Alien Spirits: Women, Men, and the Zar Cult in Northern Sudan*. Wisconsin: The University of Wisconsin Press.

———. 1992. "Comment on the Proposed DSM-IV Criteria for Trance and Possession Disorder." *Transcultural Psychiatric Research Review* 29, no. 4: 323–30.

Bourdieu, Pierre. 1977. *Outline of a Theory of Practice*. London: Cambridge University Press.

Bowen, John. 1993. *Muslims through Discourse*. Princeton: Princeton University Press.

Brown, Karen McCarthy. 1991. *Mama Lola: A Vodou Priestess in Brooklyn*. Berkeley: University of California Press.

Clifford, James, George E. Marcus, and School of American Research (Santa Fe, N.M.) 1986. *Writing Culture: The Poetics and Politics of Ethnography*. Berkeley: University of California Press.

Crain, Mary. 1991. "Poetics and Politics in the Ecuadorean Andes: Women's Narratives of Death and Devil Possession." *American Ethnologist* 18, no. 1: 67–89.

Crapanzano, Vincent. 1977a. Introduction to *Case Studies in Spirit Possession*, ed. V. Crapanzano and V. Garrison, 1–40. New York: John Wiley.

———. 1977b. "Mohammed and Dawia: Possession in Morocco." In *Case Studies in Spirit Possession*, ed. V. Crapanzano and V. Garrison, 141–76. New York: John Wiley.

———. 1980. *Tuhami: Portrait of a Moroccan*. Chicago: University of Chicago Press.

Crowfoot, Grace, and Louise Baldensperger. 1932. *From Cedar to Hyssop: A Study in the Folklore of Plants in Palestine*. London: The Sheldon Press.

Dennis, Mark. 1998. "America's Uneasy Export: It's a Hard Life for U.S. Muslims in the West Bank." *Newsweek*, March 16, 37.

el-Messiri, Sawsan. 1978. "Self-Images of Traditional Urban Women in Cairo." In *Women in the Muslim World*, ed. L. Beck and N. Keddie, 522–40. Cambridge, MA: Harvard University Press.

Escribano, Marisa. 1987. The Endurance of the Olive Tree: Tradition and Identity in Two West Bank Palestinian Villages. Ph.D. diss., Harvard University.

Foucault, Michel. 1980. *Power/Knowledge: Selected Interviews and Other Writings*, ed. C. Gordon. New York: Pantheon Press.

Geertz, Hildred. 1979. "The Meaning of Family Ties." In *Meaning and Order in Moroccan Society*, ed. C. Geertz, H. Geertz, and L. Rosen, 315–79. New York: Cambridge University Press.

Gellner, Ernest. 1981. *Muslim Society*. Cambridge: Cambridge University Press.

Giacaman, Rita, Camilla Stoltenberg, and Lars Weiseth. 1994. "Health." In *Palestinian Society in Gaza, West Bank and Arab Jerusalem: A Survey of Living Conditions*, Report 151, ed. M. Heiberg and G. Ovensen, 99–130. Ramallah: FAFO.

Gibb, Camilla, and Celia Rothenberg. 2000. "Believing Women: Harari and Palestinian Women at Home and in the Canadian Diaspora." *Journal of Muslim Minority Affairs* 20, no. 2: 243–59.

Gilbert, John P., and Eugene A. Hammel. 1966. "Computer Simulation and Analysis of Problems in Kinship and Social Structure." *American Anthropologist* 68, no 1: 71–93.

Granqvist, Hilma. 1931. *Marriage Conditions in a Palestinian Village*. Helsingfors: Societas Scientiarum Fennica.

———. 1935. *Marriage Conditions in a Palestinian Village II*. Helsingfors: Societas Scientiarum Fennica.

———. 1947. *Birth and Childhood among the Arabs*. Helsingfors: Soderstrom.

———. 1950. *Child Problems among the Arabs: Studies in a Muhammadan Village in Palestine*. Helsingfors: Soderstrom.

———. 1965. *Muslim Death and Burial*. Helsingfors: Helsinki.

Haj, Samira. 1992. "Palestinian Women and Patriarchal Relations." *Signs* 17, no 4: 761–78.

Hammami, Rema. 1990. "Women, the Hijab, and the Intifada." *Middle East Report* 164/165 (May–August): 24–28, 71, 78.

———. 1994. "Women in Palestinian Society." In *Palestinian Society in Gaza, West Bank, and Arab Jerusalem*, Report 151, ed. M. Heiberg and G. Ovensen, 283–311. Ramallah: FAFO.

Hammami, Rema, and Jamil Hilal. 2001. "An Uprising at a Crossroads." *Middle East Report* 219 (Summer): 2–7, 41.

Hecht, Esther. 1996. "Therapy for Society." *The Jerusalem Post*, July 26.

Heiberg, Marianne. 1994. "Education." In *Palestinian Society in Gaza, West Bank, and Arab Jerusalem: A Survey of Living Conditions*, Report 151, ed. M. Heiberg and G. Ovensen, 131–54. Ramallah: FAFO.

Inhorn, Marcia. 1996. *Infertility and Patriarchy: The Cultural Politics of Gender and Family Life in Egypt*. Philadelphia: University of Pennsylvania Press.

Jameson, Fredric. 1981. *The Political Unconscious: Narrative as a Socially Symbolic Act*. Ithaca, NY: Cornell University Press.

Jean-Klein, Iris. 2000. "Mothercraft, Statecraft, and Subjectivity in the Palestinian Intifada." *American Ethnologist* 27, no 1: 100–127.

Joseph, Suad. 1978. "Women and the Neighborhood Street in Borj Hammoud, Lebanon." In *Women in the Muslim World*, ed. L. Beck and N. Keddie, 541–58. Cambridge, MA: Harvard University Press.

———. 1999. "Brother–Sister Relationships." In *Intimate Selving in Arab Families: Gender, Self, and Identity*, ed. S. Joseph, 113–40. Syracuse, N.Y.: Syracuse University Press.

Kahana, Yael. 1985. "The Zar Spirits, a Category of Magic in the System of Mental Health Care in Ethiopia." *International Journal of Social Psychiatry* 31, no 2: 125–43.

Kanaaneh, Rhoda Ann. 2002. *Birthing the Nation: Strategies of Palestinian Women in Israel.* Berkeley: University of California Press.

Kanafani, Noman. 1995. "Homecoming." *Middle East Report* 194/195 (May–June/July–August): 40–42.

Khader, Hassan. 1997. "Confessions of a Palestinian Returnee." *Journal of Palestine Studies* XXVII, no 1: 85–95.

Khalidi, Muhammad. 1995. "A First Visit to Palestine." *Journal of Palestine Studies* XXIV, no 3: 74–80.

Khamal, Farid. 1974. Al-Jinn wa al-'afārīt [The Jinn and the Devils]. *Al-Funūn al-Sha'bīyya* 1, no 4: 88–95.

Khuri, Fuad. 1970. "Parallel Cousin Marriage Reconsidered: A Middle Eastern Practice that Nullifies the Effects of Marriage on the Intensity of Family Relationships." *Man* 5, no 4: 597–618.

Kulick, Don, and Margaret Willson. 1995. *Taboo: Sex, Identity, and Erotic Subjectivity in Anthropological Fieldwork.* New York: Routledge.

Lambek, Michael. 1980. "Spirits and Spouses: Possession as a System of Communication among the Malagasy Speakers of Mayotte." *American Ethnologist* 7, no 2: 318–31.

———. 1981. *Human Spirits: A Cultural Account of Trance in Mayotte.* New York: Cambridge University Press.

———. 1990. "Certain Knowledge, Contestable Authority: Power and Practice on the Islamic Periphery." *American Ethnologist* 17, no 1: 23–40.

———. 1993. *Knowledge and Practice in Mayotte: Local Discourses of Islam, Sorcery, and Spirit Possession.* Toronto: University of Toronto Press.

———. 1996. "Afterword: Spirits and Their Histories." In *Spirits in Culture, History and Mind*, ed. J. Mageo and A. Howard, 237–50. New York: Routledge.

Lewis, I. M. 1975. *Ecstatic Religion.* Harmondsworth, Middlesex, England: Penguin Books.

Lutfiyya, Abdullah. 1966. *Baytin: A Jordanian Village.* The Hague: Mouton and Company.

MacCormack, Carol, and Marily Strathern, eds. 1980. *Nature, Culture and Gender.* New York: Cambridge University Press.

Mageo, Jeanette, and Alan Howard, eds. 1996. *Spirits in Culture, History, and Mind.* New York: Routledge.

Marcus, George E., and Michael M. J. Fischer. 1986. *Anthropology as Cultural Critique: An Experimental Moment in the Human Sciences.* Chicago: University of Chicago Press.

Mattingly, Cheryl. 1998. *Healing Dramas and Clinical Plots: The Narrative Structure of Experience.* Cambridge, U.K.: Cambridge University Press.

Meneley, Anne. 1996. *Tournaments of Value: Sociability and Hierarchy in a Yemen Town.* Toronto: University of Toronto Press.

Messick, Brinkley. 1987. "Subordinate Discourse: Women, Weaving and Gender Relations in North Africa." *American Ethnologist* 14, no 2: 210–25.

Moors, Anneliese. 1995. *Women, Property and Islam: Palestinian Experiences, 1920–1990.* Cambridge, U.K.: Cambridge University Press.

Morsy, Soheir. 1991. "Spirit Possession in Egyptian Ethnomedicine: Origins, Comparison and Historical Specificity." In *Women's Medicine: The Zar-Bori Cult in Africa and Beyond,* ed. I. Lewis, A. Al-Safi, and S. Hurreiz, 189–208. Edinburgh: Edinburgh University Press.

Muhawi, Ibrahim, and Sharif Kanaana. 1989. *Speak Bird, Speak Again: Palestinian Arab Folktales.* Berkeley: University of California Press.

Murphy, Robert, and Leonard Kasdan. 1959. "The Structure of Parallel Cousin Marriage." *American Anthropologist* 61, no 1: 17–29.

Nakhleh, Khalil. 1977. "Anthropological and Sociological Studies on the Arabs in Israel: A Critique." *Journal of Palestine Studies* 6, no 4: 41–70.

Negev, Eilat. 1995. *Dybbuk Tza!* [Get Out, Dybbuk!] *Yediot Ahronot* (15 December): 70–78.

Nelson, Cynthia. 1974. "Public and Private Politics: Women in the Middle Eastern World." *American Ethnologist* 1, no 3: 551–63.

Nichter, Mark. 1981. "Idioms of Distress: Alternatives in the Expression of Psychosocial Distress: A Case Study from South India." *Culture, Medicine, and Psychiatry* 5, no 4: 379–408.

Ong, Aihwa. 1987. *Spirits of Resistance and Capitalist Discipline: Factory Women in Malaysia.* Albany: State University of New York Press.

Ovensen, Geir. 1994. "Employment and Under-Utilization of Labour." In *Palestinian Society in Gaza, West Bank, and Arab Jerusalem,* Vol. Report 151, ed. M. Heiberg and G. Ovensen, 181–220. Ramallah: FAFO.

Peled, Yoav. 1995. "From Zionism to Capitalism: The Political Economy of Israel's Decolonization of the Occupied Territories." *Middle East Report* 194/195 (May–June/July–August): 13–17.

Peteet, Julie. 1994. "Male Gender and Rituals of Resistance in the Palestinian Intifada: A Cultural Politics of Violence." *American Ethnologist* 21, no 1: 31–49.

Rabbani, Mouin. 1996. "Palestinian Authority, Israeli Rule: From Transitional to Permanent Arrangement." *Middle East Report* 201 (October–December): 2–6, 22.

Rajab, Jehan. 1989. *Palestinian Costume.* London: Kegan Paul International.

Rosaldo, Michelle. 1974. "Women, Culture, and Society: A Theoretical Overview." In *Women, Culture, and Society,* ed. M. Rosaldo and L. Lamphere, 17–42. Stanford: Stanford University Press.

Rosaldo, Michelle, and Louise Lamphere, eds. 1974. *Women, Culture, and Society.* Stanford: Stanford University Press.

Rosen, Lawrence. 2002. *The Culture of Islam: Changing Aspects of Contemporary Muslim Life.* Chicago: University of Chicago Press.

Rosenfeld, Henry. 1960. "On Determinants of the Status of Arab Village Women." *Man* 60: 66–70.

———. 1964. "From Peasantry to Wage Labour and Residual Peasantry: The Transformation of an Arab Village." In *Process and Pattern in Culture,* ed. R. Manners, 211–34. Chicago: Aldine.

——. 1968. "Change, Barriers to Change, and Contradictions in the Arab Village Family." *American Anthropologist* 70, no 4: 732–52.

Rothenberg, Celia. 1999a. "Who Are We For Them? On Doing Research in the Palestinian West Bank." In *Feminist Fields: Ethnographic Insights*, ed. R. Bridgman, S. Cole, and H. Howard-Bobiwash, 137–56. Peterborough, Ontario: Broadview Press.

——. 1999b. "Proximity and Distance: Palestinian Women's Social Lives in Diaspora." *Diaspora: A Journal of Transnational Studies* 8, no 1: 23–50.

——. 1998–1999. "A Review of the Anthropological Literature in English on the Palestinian Hamula and Women." *The Journal of Arabic and Islamic Studies* II: 24–48, http://www.uib.no/jais/content2.html

Rubenberg, Cheryl A. 2001. *Palestinian Women: Patriarchy and Resistance in the West Bank*. Boulder: Lynne Reinner Publishers.

Ruggi, Suzanne. 1998. "Commodifying Honor in Female Sexuality: Honor Killings in Palestine." *Middle East Report* 206 (Spring): 12–15.

Saleh, Mustafa. 1975. al-Qirā'a al-Tali' [Fortune Telling]. *Al-Funūn al-Sha'bīyya* 2, no 3: 98–105.

Schmoll, Pamela. 1993. "Black Stomachs, Beautiful Stones: Soul-Eating among Hausa in Niger." In *Modernity and Its Malcontents*, ed. J. Comaroff and J. Comaroff, 193–220. Chicago: University of Chicago Press.

Schneider, David M. 1980. *American Kinship: A Cultural Account*. Chicago: University of Chicago Press.

Seger, Karen. 1981. *Portrait of a Palestinian Village*. London: Third World Centre for Research and Publishing.

Sered, Susan. 1994. *Priestess, Mother, Sacred Sister*. New York: Oxford University Press.

Shavit, Ari. 2002. "No Man's Land: The Idea of a City Disappears." *The New Yorker* (December 9): 56–60.

Shehadeh, Raja. 1995. "Transfers and Powers: The August Agreement and the Jordanian Option." *Middle East Report* 194/195 (May–August): 29–32.

Sherwell, Tina. 1996. "Palestinian Costume, the Intifada, and the Gendering of Nationalist Discourse." *Journal of Gender Studies* 5, no 3: 293–303.

Swedenburg, Ted. 1989. "Occupational Hazards: Palestine Ethnography." *Cultural Anthropology* 4, no 3: 265–72.

——. 1990. "The Palestinian Peasant as National Signifier." *Anthropological Quarterly* 63: 18–30.

Tamari, Salim and Rema Hammami. 1998. "Virtual Returns to Jaffa." *Journal of Palestine Studies* XXVII, no 4: 65–79.

Tapper, Nancy, and Richard Tapper. 1987. "The Birth of the Prophet: Ritual and Gender in Turkish Islam." *Man* 22, no 1: 69–92

Taussig, Michael. 1980. "Reification and the Consciousness of the Patient." *Social Science and Medicine* 14B: 3–13.

United Nations Relief and Works Agency for Palestine Refugees in the Near East. 1996. Map of Area of Operations (June 30).

Weir, Shelagh. 1989. *Palestinian Costume*. London: British Museum Publications.

Weston, Kath. 1995. "Forever Is a Long Time: Romancing the Real in Gay Kinship Ideologies." In *Naturalizing Power: Essays in Feminist Cultural Analysis*, ed. S. Yanagisako and C. Delaney, 87–112. New York: Routledge.

Widen, Solveig. 1998. "Alma Soderhjelm and Hilma Granqvist." *Gender and History* 10, no 1: 133–42.

Wikan, Unni. 1982. *Behind the Veil in Arabia: Women in Oman.* Chicago: University of Chicago Press.

Wolf, Diane. 1996. *Feminist Dilemmas in Fieldwork.* Boulder: Westview Press.

Ya'ari, Ehud. 1989. "Israel's Prison Academies." *The Atlantic* 274 (October): 22–30.

Yanagisako, Sylvia, and Carol Delaney. 1995. "Naturalizing Power." In *Naturalizing Power: Essays in Feminist Cultural Analysis*, ed. S. Yanagisako and C. Delaney, 1–24. New York: Routledge.

Yanagisako, Sylvia, and Jane Collier. 1987. "Toward a Unified Analysis of Gender and Kinship." In *Gender and Kinship: Essays toward a Unified Analysis*, ed. J. Collier and S. Yanagisako, 14–50. Stanford: Stanford University Press.

Index

diaspora, 86, 108–11
dybbuk, 94

education, 57–58, 75n3, 75n4
el-Messiri, Sawsan, 26n7
El-Sohl, Camillia Fawzi, 15
epilepsy, 42, 44
Escribano, Marisa, 75n2, 124

FAFO survey, 13, 19, 57
family relationships, 10–11, 123–25
FBD marriage. *See* marriage, to cousin
finjān, 47
Fischer, Michael M. J., 15
folk tales, 8
fortune telling, 46–48
Fosta, 14, 106, 115, 121n2
Foucault, Michel, 7
four mountains, 20–25

Gaza Community Mental Health
    Program, 43, 44
Geertz, Hildred, 11, 26n8, 134
Gellner, Ernest, 128
Giacaman, Rita, 13
Gibb, Camilla, 17
Gilbert, John P., 98
Gordon, Deborah A., 15
Granqvist, Hilma, 2, 3, 13, 15, 20, 25n2,
    26n11, 29–35, 84, 85, 86, 97n2,
    98n3, 98n4, 98n6, 133, 135
the Great Tradition, 128

Haj, Samira, 124
Halah, 59–61
Hamid, 101
Hammami, Rema, 24, 41, 56, 75n1, 108
Hammel, Eugene A., 98
ḥamūla, 10, 123–24
ḥāra, 10, 11, 124
Hassan and Ghada, 107–15
Hebrew, speaking, 91–93, 112
Hecht, Esther, 43, 44
Heiberg, Marianne, 26n13, 57
Hilal, Jamil, 24

honor killing, 63
Howard, Alan, 9

ibn balad, 10, 88
Ibrahim, 102–5
identity in fieldwork, 15–17
illocutionary acts, 65
infertility, 65–70, 126
Inhorn, Marcia, 126
insanity, 45
isolation, 108–9
Israeli occupation, 11, 21, 24, 86–87,
    94, 100, 124, 127

Jameson, Fredric, 9
Jean-Klein, Iris, 100
The Jerusalem Post, 43
Jewish jinn, 36, 77, 90–94, 100, 102–4
Jewish possession by spirits, 94–96
jinn: animal form, 33, 35, 51n4;
    appearance of, 33, 35, 51n4, 103,
    121n1; changes in, 35–36;
    contemporary, 35–36; conversion of,
    39; as discourse, 7–9, 13, 25n6;
    evil/good nature of, 32, 101, 102;
    forms of, 33, 35, 51n4; fortune
    telling and, 46–48; historical
    precedent for, 29–51; illness and, 14,
    34; Israeli use of, 99–100; Jewish,
    36, 77, 90–94, 100, 102–4; marriage
    to, 107–15; and men, 14, 37, 99–120,
    130, 131; origins of, 30, 51n2;
    physical effects of, 14; political
    beliefs and, 106; in prisons, 99–120;
    protection from, 30, 31; social
    geography and, 123–32; stories, 7–9,
    13, 25n6; today, 35–36; "wearing,"
    2, 6–7; and women, 37, 53–75,
    128–30, 131. *See also* possession
jinnia, 14, 102–5, 106–15
Joseph, Suad, 10, 26n9, 84

Kahana, Yael, 36, 51n2, 90
Kanaana, Sharif, 8
Kanaaneh, Rhoda Ann, 68, 128

qaraba, 26n8
qarīb, 9, 10, 26n8
quraba, 26n8
Qu'ran, and treatment of possession, 38, 39, 42, 60, 61

Rabbani, Mouin, 22, 23, 24
Rabin, Yitzhak, assassination of, 21–22
Rajab, Jehan, 2
Rosaldo, Michelle, 34, 125, 126
Rosen, Lawrence, 51n3
Rosenfeld, Henry, 98n3, 124
Rothenberg, Celia, 15, 17, 26n10
Rubenberg, Cheryl A., 63, 124
Ruggi, Suzanne, 63

Sa'ida, 66–70
Saleh, Mustafa, 47, 52n12
Samaritans, as specialists in jinn treatment, 52n10
Samira, 70–74
Sanad, Musa, 5, 17, 18, 19–20, 29, 135
Sara, 62
Sarraj, Eyad, 43–44
Schmoll, Pamela, 52n6
Schneider, David M., 11
Seger, Karen, 25n2
Sered, Susan, 128, 129, 130
sexuality and the jinn, 30, 31, 33, 35
sharaf al-bint, 63
Shavit, Ari, 22
Shehadeh, Raja, 21
Sherwell, Tina, 4
shughl, 58, 68, 73
sibrna, 2
social geography: family relationships, 10–11, 123–25; friendships, 11–12, 124–25; marriage, 83–89; morality, 125–27; overview, 9–12; proximity, 9–10, 18, 26n9, 105; religious

beliefs, 127–30; social space, 125–27
social space, morality and, 120, 125–27
Stoltenberg, Camilla, 13
Strathern, Marilyn, 125
Swedenburg, Ted, 25n5, 25n6

Tamari, Salim, 108
Tapper, Nancy, 128
Tapper, Richard, 128
tatriz, 59
Taussig, Michael, 45
tawjihi, 57
thōb, 2, 4, 5

United Nations Relief and Works Agency for Palestine Refugees in the Near East, 27n16
unmarried women, 55–59, 59–61, 62

virginity, loss of, 63–65

"wearing" the jinn, 2, 6–7
Weir, Shelagh, 2, 4
Weston, Kath, 11
Widen, Solveig, 26n11
Wikan, Unni, 26n9, 51
Wilson, Margaret, 15
Wolf, Diane, 15
women: bodies, 93–94; and the jinn, 37, 53–75, 128–30, 131; piety of, 74; as religious leaders, 41; unmarried, 55–57, 59–61, 62
women's work, 72–74
wusikh, 56, 75n2

Ya'ari, Ehud, 100
Yanagisako, Sylvia, 35, 124

Zahia, 77–97
zar, 36

About the Author

Celia Rothenberg is assistant professor of religious studies and health studies at McMaster University. Her research interests include the relationships among religion, health, and healing in Canada and the Middle East.

CPSIA information can be obtained at www.ICGtesting.com
Printed in the USA
BVOW04s2134211016

465734BV00001B/40/P